TSUMI
AND OHNO KAZUO

D0994147

Routledge Performance Practitioners is a series of introductory guides to the key theatre-makers of the last century. Each volume explains the background to and the work of one of the major influences on twentieth- and twenty-first-century performance.

These compact, well-illustrated and clearly written books unravel the contribution of modern theatre's most charismatic innovators. *Hijikata Tatsumi and Ohno Kazuo* is the first book to combine:

- an account of the founding of Japanese butoh through the partnership of Hijikata and Ohno, extending to the larger story of butoh's international assimilation
- an exploration of the impact of the social and political issues of post-World War II Japan on the aesthetic development of butoh
- metamorphic dance experiences that students of butoh can explore
- a glossary of English and Japanese terms.

As a first step towards critical understanding, and as an initial exploration before going on to further, primary research, **Routledge Performance Practitioners** are unbeatable value for today's student.

Sondra Fraleigh is Professor Emeritus of dance and somatic studies at the State University of New York at Brockport.

Tamah Nakamura is a Professor at Chikushi Jogakuen University, Fukuoka, Japan, a somatic movement educator and butoh dancer.

ROUTLEDGE PERFORMANCE PRACTITIONERS

Series editor: Franc Chamberlain, University College Cork

Routledge Performance Practitioners is an innovative series of introductory handbooks on key figures in twentieth-century performance practice. Each volume focuses on a theatre-maker whose practical and theoretical work has in some way transformed the way we understand theatre and performance. The books are carefully structured to enable the reader to gain a good grasp of the fundamental elements underpinning each practitioner's work. They will provide an inspiring springboard for future study, unpacking and explaining what can initially seem daunting.

The main sections of each book cover:

* personal biography
* explanation of key writings
* description of significant productions
* reproduction of practical exercises.

Volumes currently available in the series are:

Eugenio Barba by Jane Turner
Augusto Boal by Frances Babbage
Michael Chekhov by Franc Chamberlain
Jacques Copeau by Mark Evans
Anna Halprin by Libby Worth and Helen Poyner
Jacques Lecoq by Simon Murray
Joan Littlewood by Nadine Holdsworth
Vsevolod Meyerhold by Jonathan Pitches
Konstantin Stanislavsky by Bella Merlin
Hijikata Tatsumi and Ohno Kazuo by Sondra Fraleigh and
    Tamah Nakamura

Future volumes will include:

Antonin Artaud	*Rudolf Laban*
Pina Bausch	*Robert Lepage*
Bertolt Brecht	*Ariane Mnouchkine*
Peter Brook	*Lee Strasberg*
Etienne Decroux	*Mary Wigman*
Jerzy Grotowski	*Robert Wilson*

HIJIKATA TATSUMI AND OHNO KAZUO

Sondra Fraleigh
and Tamah Nakamura

Routledge
Taylor & Francis Group

NEW YORK AND LONDON

First published 2006
by Routledge
270 Madison Ave, New York, NY 10016

Simultaneously published in the UK
by Routledge
2 Park Square, Milton Park, Abingdon, Oxon OX14 4RN

*Routledge is an imprint of the Taylor & Francis Group,
an informa business*

© 2006 Sondra Fraleigh and Tamah Nakamura

Typeset in Perpetua by
Book Now Ltd

British Library Cataloguing in Publication Data
A catalogue record for this book is available from
the British Library

Library of Congress Cataloging in Publication Data
Fraleigh, Sondra Horton, 1939–
Hijikata Tatsumi and Ohno Kazuo/Sondra Fraleigh and Tamah
    Nakamura. – 1st ed.
        p. cm. – (Routledge performance practitioners)
    Includes bibliographical references and index.
    1. Butō. 2. Modern dance–Japan. I. Nakamura, Tamah. II. Title.
III. Series.
GV1783.2.B87F735 2006
792.80952–dc22   2005034721

ISBN10: 0–415–35438–2 (hbk)
ISBN10: 0–415–35439–0 (pbk)
ISBN10: 0–203–00103–6 (ebk)

ISBN13: 978–0–415–35438–7 (hbk)
ISBN13: 978–0–415–35439–2 (pbk)
ISBN13: 978–0–203–00103–5 (ebk)

CONTENTS

FIGURES

ACKNOWLEDGMENTS

We wish to thank those scholars whose past work on butoh has made this work possible, especially Goda Nario, Ichikawa Miyabi, Kurihara Nanako, Mikami Kayo, Bruce Baird, Kasai Toshiharu, Susan Klein, Kuniyoshi Kazuko, Joan Laage, Lizzie Slater, Tachiki Takashi, Jean Viala, Nourit Masson-Sekine, Tachiki Akiko, Yoshioka Minoru, and Kurt Wurmli. Ohno Yoshito's writings on his father Kazuo's work, as they also reflect his dances with Kazuo and Hijikata, greatly aid our portrait of these men. We are also grateful to Ohno Yoshito for his interview with Tamah Nakamura in preparation for this book.

We are indebted to the many butoh performers and teachers who have furthered our understanding of this unique dance genre and its founders. It was Nakajima Natsu who first introduced Sondra Fraleigh to butoh and to Ohno Kazuo, and Mikami Kayo introduced Fraleigh to the workshops of Ashikawa Yoko in Tokyo. Harada Nobuo introduced Tamah Nakamura to butoh through workshops and performances in her hometown of Fukuoka, Japan. Nakamura is also grateful to archivists Morishita Takashi and Murai Takemi of Keio University Research Center for the Arts & Arts Administration, Tokyo, for their generous assistance in locating resources on the history of butoh and for their extensive explanations. Our connections to various artists and scholars of butoh appear throughout the book, particularly in the last chapter on butoh explorations. We especially thank those artists who generously contributed their workshop words to this chapter: Nakajima Natsu, Ohno Yoshito, Yoshioka Yumiko, Morita Itto, Takeuchi Mika, Takenouchi Atsushi, Frances Barbe, and Harada Nobuo. We also acknowledge Waguri Yukio whose CD-Rom of Hijikata's *butoh-fu* (dance notations, butoh words and images) is invaluable to any understanding of Hijikata's work. A special mention for the photographs goes to Morishita Takashi of the Hijikata Tatsumi Archives, Keio University Research Center for the Arts & Arts Administration, Tokyo and Mizohata Toshio of the Ohno Dance Studio Archives, Yokohama.

A special thanks to Tamah Nakamura's husband Yoshihiro, professor of linguistics, who has supported this work with his bilingual expertise and his generous spirit. His original translations of a portion of Ohno Kazuo's *butoh-fu* appear in Chapter 2.

NOTE ON NAMES AND GLOSSARIES

For Japanese names we have chosen the Japanese convention of using the last name first. Thus Hijikata Tatsumi appears with the surname first and the personal name second. English language names retain the familiar form of first name followed by surname.

Butoh in its genesis has interesting ties to European dance, theater, and visual arts, as well as other cultural sources. Several aesthetic and literary movements having their origins in the nineteenth and early twentieth century are involved, such as surrealism, existentialism, and expressionism. We explain terms that might be new to some readers briefly as they come up, but find it necessary to provide a fuller definition of key concepts and central figures in the history of butoh. These appear in the English Glossary of Terms. We have also provided a Japanese Glossary of Terms in a list format, so that English-speaking students of butoh can see the romanization of butoh terms next to the original Japanese ideograms. These can stimulate the imagination, as they have their origins in brush stroke calligraphy and give an immediate picture of a word.

INTRODUCTION

This work gives an account of Hijikata Tatsumi and Ohno Kazuo, telling the story of the founding of Japanese butoh through their partnership as performers and choreographers, extending to the larger story of butoh's international assimilation. It also weaves the aesthetic development of butoh with the social and political issues of post-World War II Japan. *Bu* means dance and *to* means step. Most simply speaking, butoh is a dance step; also known as Ankoku Butoh – darkness dance. The dance begun by Hijikata and Ohno is now identified as "butoh" (sometimes "buto") and practiced around the globe. For contemporary dancers in the lineage of Hijikata and Ohno, butoh is still dark, but not entirely; bodies of light often ensue from darkness, as in Takenouchi Atsushi's *Jinen Butoh* – dance with nature. Keenly aware of the strictures of society, Hijikata wanted to uncover the dance already happening in the body. As one of his many inheritors, Takenouchi works with a similar principle: "everything is already dancing" (Takenouchi, Interview with Fraleigh, 2003).

Originally an underground movement in Japan, butoh emerged in the aftermath of World War II. It is sometimes interpreted as post-atomic spectacle, but this would be too simple an explanation for this enigmatic art. If Hijikata sometimes dances the crucified martyr, his dance does not reduce to sympathy or guilt. No master key unlocks his creative motivations, but he was undoubtedly aware of his unique place in history. Protest against the Westernization of Japan compelled

Hijikata's butoh in part; he rejected Western dominion and sought a dance that would be true to his ethnic roots and Japanese body. The United States dropped atomic bombs on Hiroshima and Nagasaki in 1945 – shaking history in an instant – and spreading American power in Japan. It was just less than a hundred years since American Commodore Matthew C. Perry in 1853 with a letter from President Millard Fillmore had sailed his tar-covered ships into Tokyo Bay, ordering Japan's ports open to international trade, at cannon point. America's actions were driven by its desire to trade, to spread the gospel to the yellow pagans, and export American democracy (Toland 1970: 54). In a very short time, a medieval Japan moved from three hundred years of self-chosen isolation into a rapidly modernizing world, and the Japanese began to imitate American and European forceful diplomacy.

"I do not want a bad check called democracy," was Hijikata's response to the encroachment of the West after World War II. He thought of his dance as "human rehabilitation," a "purposeless non-product" in protest of the rise of capitalist production in Japan. Butoh finally did include the West, however. As it looked back to rescue Japanese identity, it also gestured toward the future, and it connected with the European arts of surrealism and expressionism. But it is most significant to an under-standing of the global climate of butoh that Japan had already influenced these art and literary movements in Europe, beginning sequentially with impressionism and symbolism in the late nineteenth century and moving into the twentieth century toward surrealism and expressionism. Europe and America appropriated many art techniques from Japan and learned from them – as we will explore. Come full circle, the art and poetry of surrealism and existentialist Theater of the Absurd inspired Hijikata's invention of butoh. He also studied with proponents of expressionist dance, known as Neue Tanz in Germany and sometimes referred to as *Poison Dance* in Japan.

During a frustrating period in his dance career, Hijikata saw Ohno, twenty years his senior, dance. He was captivated with Ohno's expres-siveness: "For years the drug of Ohno stayed in my memory," Hijikata wrote. Together Hijikata and Ohno would reject the ballet and modern dance of the West and champion a new dance that rescued "the Japanese body" on ethnographic grounds, also showing odd ticks, shaking, and exposing facial transformations, from sublime to ridiculous. Meta-morphosis became a butoh signature. Thus in the last chapter, we will explore metamorphic butoh practice.

The dance of Hijikata and Ohno spanned national distinctions – it was so close to the awkward, eloquent, gestural body that communicates intrinsically. Butoh's irrational character and its rejection of social mores made it a difficult art for many, however. Shaped in the politics of identity, butoh flourished underground in Tokyo before it became an international phenomenon. In contrast to the formalist tendencies of American postmodern dance, butoh reveals expression, and many of its practices attend directly to community building through amateur participation. Butoh crosses into dance therapy as well because of its acceptance of imperfection. "Start from the place of your handicap," Hijikata's female counterpart Ashikawa Yoko liked to say in her butoh classes, echoing her years with Hijikata.

The chaotic post-war climate of Japan prefigured the growth of butoh as a postmodern and primal form of dance with therapeutic potential. Hijikata's identification with the poverty of his homeland, Tohoku, and his radical use of nativism, popular in 1970s Japan, entered directly into his highly original, comic, painful, and empathetic dance. On the other hand, Ohno developed a spiritual, often delicate and poetic improvisational style. Through the structural, choreographed, butoh of Hijikata and the free, improvisational butoh of Ohno, a new art form with a wide range of aesthetic possibilities entered the lexicon of theater arts in Japan and abroad, also affecting visual art and photography.

Like the implausible Zen-sound of one hand clapping, butoh has provocative aims. As is often the case in dance, choreographic intent is one thing, but the far-reaching consequences that arise between the dancer and the witness can surpass the original intent. Audiences are people; they experience the dance through their own identity and history. Ohno points toward this interactive aspect of dance in his hope that the audience will give back something unexpected from his performances (Fraleigh 1999: 162). Ashikawa, the female founder of butoh, believes that the audience will enter into the imagistic process of butoh, even if they do not identify each image exactly (Ibid. 142). She practiced butoh through her embodiment of surrealist imagery, emptying herself to become a vessel for Hijikata's inventive, irreconcilable butoh-fu – poetic word images he generated for butoh movement and gestures, sometimes referred to as notation since they are used to guide and inspire dance movement. So what does butoh mean (or what do *butoh-fu* communicate)? Butoh dancers might say "nothing," and they would be both right and wrong. Butoh, even more than other dance, befuddles the rational mind, not communicating denotative discrete meaning; rather it survives on images that continually change, riding the moment of meaning in transition.

Butoh has global implications as it morphs from image to image and across cultures, releasing freedom of engagement for the audience. If it survives with some specificity, it will continue to be identified in ever-new contexts. If not a direct result of the atomic bomb, butoh is nevertheless a responsive post-war art, and the bomb was more than just a blast. As an ultimatum in respect for cultural differences, the bomb and its unlearned lessons reach far into the future. When the world bears a single political stamp, it will be gone – or maybe like Hijikata, just a sole, surreal dead body standing desperately upright.

BUTOH
SHAPESHIFTERS

KAZE DARUMA: THE ORIGINS OF BUTOH

We begin with a definition: In Japan, a Daruma *is a limbless figure (or doll) weighted so that it bounces back when knocked over. It is a symbol of persistence leading to success.* Daruma *is also an abbreviation for* Bodhidharma, *a mythical Middle Eastern priest said to have carried Buddhist practice and teachings to China about 500 BC. From there, the teachings traveled to Korea in AD 372 and eventually to Japan. Prince Shōtoku proclaimed it the state religion of Japan in AD 594.*

In February of 1985, the night before the Tokyo *Butoh Festival 85* and one year before his death, Hijikata Tatsumi gave a lecture at Asahi Hall called *Kaze Daruma* (Wind Daruma), quoting an ancient Buddhist priest, Kyogai, and then telling stories of harsh winters in his homeland of Akita where *darumas* come rolling in the wind with their bones on fire. When the *Wind Daruma* stands at the door and goes into the parlor, "this is already *butoh*," Hijikata says. He remembers how as a child in the country of snow and mud he was made to eat pieces of half-burnt coal, which were supposed to cure him of "peevishness." Then he spoke about *Showa* the third [1928], the year of his birth and harbinger to war "when the Asian sky was gradually, eerily becoming overcast" (Hijikata 2000d: 74). The *Showa* period of Japanese history [1926–1988] coincides with Hijikata's life span [1928–1986]. The Japanese era designation indicating an emperor's life span started in 645, and is used in conjunction with the Christian calendar.

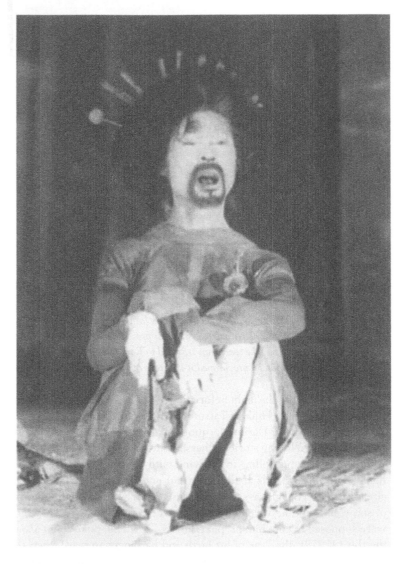

Figure 1.1 Hijikata Tatsumi in *Calm House*. Photograph by Torii Ryozen.
Courtesy the Hijikata Tatsumi Archive

In his lifetime, Hijikata witnessed Japan's military build up preceding World War II and its post-war Westernization. He experienced Japan's defeat and drastic changes in political and social values – growing to extremes in the 1960s. No area of Japanese life was immune to the political shifts taking place around the world at this time. In 1968, the year of Hijikata's dance *Revolt of the Flesh*, Japanese youths, like those in America and Europe, took to the streets in unprecedented numbers. Hijikata's theatrical revolution, while not a declared movement of The New Left, nevertheless resembled the politics of public protest. Meanwhile, under American protectionism after the war, economic growth incomparable in world history placed Japan as one of the world's major economic powers.

This is the historical crucible that tested Hijikata and marked his butoh. During the war, he languished as a lonely adolescent in a house with a lot of empty rooms with his five older brothers off in the army (2000d: 73). He began his study of modern dance in 1946 during the difficult aftermath of occupation, as Japan recovered from near collapse with America's fire bombing of Tokyo claiming as many lives as the atomic bombs dropped on Hiroshima and Nagasaki; at least 300,000 were killed, and that many more were doomed. Hijikata would eventually originate a radically new form of dance theater, *Ankoku Butoh* (darkness dance), gestating in the early post-war era and finally coming to attention during the global upheavals and political riots of the 1960s. His dance, now known simply as *butoh* (dance step), flourished underground in Tokyo, and eventually resounded around the globe in dance, theater, visual art, and photography.

Rustic and contemporary, as Western as it is Eastern, the butoh legacy of Hijikata spans cultural divides. Honed from personal and inter-cultural resources, butoh mines identity, even as it reaches beyond its local beginnings. Retention of identity amid synthesis has been the Japanese way for centuries. Likewise, it is a butoh strategy – growing at first from Hijikata's dissatisfaction with Western ballet. He finally understood in the 1950s after studying ballet for several years that his own body was not suited to this Western form. He was not innately plastic and flowing in ballet, but rather bow-legged and tense. In time, he was to turn this liability into an asset, creating out of the well of his frustration; turning first to the Japan of his rural roots, Hijikata began to work with the givens of his own body.

He also developed an absurdist, surrealist philosophy that flaunted societal taboos. His first experiment in butoh, *Kinjiki*, performed for the Japanese Dance Association 'New Face Performance' in 1959 in Tokyo, was based on the homoerotic novel *Kinjiki* (Forbidden Colors) by Mishima Yukio (1951) and featured a chicken being squeezed between the legs of Ohno Yoshito, the very young son of Ohno Kazuo (b. 1906). The elder Ohno later became a butoh icon and one of the most treasured Japanese performers of the twentieth century. The stage was dark and the dance was short, but its sexual message shocked the All Japan Art Dance Association (the name was later changed to Japan Dance Association). Some accounts say Hijikata was expelled from the association over this dance, but in fact he voluntarily resigned along with Ohno and their friend Tsuda. Hijikata's early subversive themes were drawn from the writings of Jean Genet that he read in the mid-1950s – *The Thief's Journal* (1949) and *Our Lady of Flowers* (1944) – just translated into Japanese. He even performed for a while under the stage name of Hijikata Genet. In his one program note for *Kinjiki*, Hijikata says, "I studied under Ando Mitsuko, consider Ohno Kazuo a brother, and adore Saint Genet" (Hijikata 1959).

Goda Nario wrote of *Kinjiki:*

> It made those of us who watched it to the end shudder, but once the shudder passed through our bodies, it resulted in a refreshing sense of release. Perhaps there was a darkness concealed within our bodies similar to that found in *Forbidden Colors* and which therefore responded to it with a feeling of liberation.
>
> (Goda 1983: unpaginated)

Hijikata's work eventually gained audiences in the Tokyo avant-garde, as he drew inspiration from such diverse sources as the films of Kurosawa Akira – *Yoidore Tenshi* (The Drunken Angel) – and European surrealist writers.

HIJIKATA'S BUTOH

In 1968, Hijikata choreographed one of his most quoted works – *Hijikata Tatsumi to nihonjin: Nikutai no hanran* (Hijikata Tatsumi and the Japanese: Rebellion of the Body). This work, also known as *Revolt of the Flesh*, marks Hijikata's shamanistic descent to darkness and clearly establishes a new form of dance rooted in his memories of Tohoku, the rustic landscape of his childhood in a poor district of Japan. In *Revolt,* Hijikata casts spells as his body morphs through shocking juxtapositions, twitching trance-like in a G-string beside a dangling rabbit on a pole. He gyrates and provokes with a large strapped-on golden penis, dances in a dress, swings on a rope with white cloth trailing and wrapping his hips, then surrenders himself, Christ-like, in crucifixion. Over ten years on the fringes of Tokyo's postwar modernization, Hijikata creates a radically new form of Dance Theater, merging the universal spectacle of the naked human body, stooped postures of old people in his homeland, the pain of his childhood, and his distrust of Western ways as they enter Japan through the American occupation after World War II (see Fraleigh 2005: 328). "One thing for sure," he writes in 'To Prison' in 1961, "I will no longer be cheated by a bad check called democracy. . . . Is there any greater misery than entrusting a dream to a reality from which one will sometime have to wake?" (2000b: 43).

Butoh gained a following in Japan and internationally as Hijikata's repertoire and his collaborators expanded. Through his association with Ohno Kazuo and his female protégé, Ashikawa Yoko, butoh moved from a phallocentric aesthetic to a full spectrum dance form with permeable boundaries. In 1954 the young Hijikata began lifetime collaboration with Ohno who was already middle-aged and a leader of modern dance in Japan. Ohno had studied with Eguchi Takaya who in turn was a pupil of Mary Wigman in Dresden, Germany before World War II, but Ohno turned away from Western modern dance through his work with Hijikata. Through his world tours and generous nature, Ohno won international audiences while assimilating the other, dancing *Admiring La Argentina* in a flamenco style and French painter Monet's *Water Lilies* in an impressionist one. Ohno performed his poetic butoh around the world. Hijikata never left Japan (Fraleigh 2005: 328).

Ashikawa became the third founder of butoh through her work with Hijikata beginning in 1966. Exploring the watery soma of infancy and bodily discovery, she flowed through Hijikata's word imagery in poetic streams, pouring her body through Hijikata's profuse kinesthetic images – his *butoh-fu*. He numbered and classified these; thus, while butoh remains a poetic, intuitive form of theater, it also has structure through Hijikata's imagistic and verbal notation for motivating dance (see Stewart on structure of butoh, 1998: 45-8). Today there are continuing themes of butoh, reminders of Hijikata, scattered around the globe.

Figure 1.2
Ashikawa Yoko in
Lover of Mr Bakke,
choreographed
by Hijikata.
Photograph by
Onozuka Makoto.
Courtesy the
Hijikata Tatsumi
Archive

NATURE, MUD, AND BUTOH MORPHOLOGY

Tsuchi kara umareta (I come from the mud).

Hijikata Tatsumi

Butoh can be traced to at least three major sources: Hijikata's memorial to mud and wind in his published speech '*Kaze Daruma*' outlines his somatic intimacy with nature, and casts butoh first as a unique type of performed ecological knowledge with agricultural roots. Secondly, Hijikata's development of butoh in the East/West atmosphere of Tokyo as it modernized after the war lends his dance political, cross-cultural, and urban juxtapositions (Fraleigh 2005: 327). Thirdly, Hijikata's butoh connects to the Japanese traditional arts, especially early Kabuki of the *Edo* period, in which social outcasts were believed to have special access to magic and the world of the dead. He often spoke of his desire to create a Tohoku Kabuki, reinstating the raw power of the bawdy beginnings of Kabuki while it was still a reactive art close to the folk and not yet cleaned-up for the West. White rice-powder painting of the face and body create ghostly appearances in butoh aesthetics as evolved in the work of Hijikata's disciples, subliminal reminders of the ghosts of Kabuki and Noh Theater, even though we know that Hijikata distanced himself from traditional and classical theater, both East and West. White faces and bodies link to Japan's traditional aesthetics, but in butoh these come paradoxically in the guise of darkness. Perhaps the best-known contemporary butoh company in this respect is the polished and popular Sankai Juku, grounded spiritually in the pre-history of the body, as conceived by choreographer Amagatsu Ushio.

Today's butoh dancers are still plastered with mud or offset with chalky white, as they were in Hijikata's day. The same bodies can also shine in glowing theatrical metamorphosis. Butoh can be plain and simple: still, slow, and stark. As Japan's most prominent performance export, butoh is deconstructive in its own way: "The body that becomes" is the ontic, metamorphic signature of butoh aesthetics, recently sustaining new permutations like MoBu — blending modern dance with butoh stylizations. Butoh's deconstructive tendencies can be wild in ways the West does not often associate with the East — free and uninhibited, nude and raw. Butoh can also be understated and smooth, cultivating small details of movement in facial expressions that move and melt sublimely (Ibid. 337). The refractive imagery of butoh does not idealize nature,

Figure 1.3
Ohno in his modern dance days, before going to war. Courtesy Ohno Kazuo Archive

nor does it present human nature as such. Rather butoh dancers expose multiple natures as they become insects, or struggle to stand upright and pass through states of dissolution as in Hijikata's famous "Ash Pillar" process. As pillars of ash, dancers enter the paradox of themselves, struggling for presence while disintegrating.

Contradicting the balanced essence of ballet, butoh plies the excitement of being off-balance, and the psychic path of shaking and plodding. Its somatic subtly goes to hair-splitting extremes. Takeuchi Mika and Morita Itto who base their butoh therapy in the movement work of Noguchi Michizo teach that what you experience depends upon how well you discern "hair-splitting" minute differences. Characterized by subtle change, butoh is not one thing: Morphing faces, states of limbo and contradiction, mark its beautiful ugliness. A dance film made in the 1960s by Hosoe Eikoh featuring Hijikata and his wife Motofuji Akiko, *Heso to Genbaku* (Navel and Atomic Bomb) is an early example of butoh metamorphosis or "the body that becomes," also grasped in the irreconcilable poetics of Hijikata as "the nature that bleeds." Morphing, melting figures permeate butoh. Their meaning is not literal but ongoing and open to interpretation.

Although Hijikata disavowed religion, the irrational non-doing of Zen, deeply embedded in the quietude of Japan, is subtext in much butoh. In his final workshop, Hijikata encouraged students to disperse into "nothingness" – quite a Buddhist ruse. Kasai Akira, who danced with Hijikata in the formative years of butoh, states that surrealism and the theater of the absurd influenced Hijikata early in his career (Fraleigh 1999: 232). Hijikata's search for a Japanese identity resulted in surreal (or disorienting) aesthetic features of butoh techniques. The butoh aesthetic loops historically from Japan to the West, and goes back to Japan. More recently it reaches out internationally toward a "community body" of floating and gravitational powers in the work of Kasai (Ibid. 247–9), while the *Jinen Butoh* of Takenouchi Atsushi approaches the aura of death chambers and the far-reaching effects of nuclear fallout – dancing on the killing fields of war.

BUTOH ALCHEMY IN GLOBAL CIRCULATION

As their butoh grew through the latter part of the twentieth century, Hijikata and Ohno rejected the theater dance of their time, whether modern or traditional – American, European, or Japanese. It is possible, nevertheless, to trace butoh's influences back to the original expressionist "stew" of modern dance in the 1920s and 1930s, and to discern traditional Japanese aesthetics in butoh as well: from the theatrical flair of Kabuki and inscrutable slowness of Noh to the exaggerations of physique and stylized facial expressions in Ukiyo-e color prints. Butoh is based on individual experiment, the same faith in intuitively derived movement and improvisatory exploration that fueled the expressionist beginnings of modern dance. But butoh differs from earlier dance experiments through its inclusive return to Japanese folk roots, while at the same time exposing a postmodern jumble of cross-cultural currents, just as Tokyo itself meshes East and West in its post-war culture, and throughout Japan, one can find amazing aesthetic assimilation: ornate Chinese temples, Indian yoga, religious practices from around the world, European fashions, kimonos and Western business suits in the streets, expensive Swiss-like ski resorts with outdoor Japanese baths, American popular culture everywhere, Disneyland and Zen amidst the celebrations of Christmas (Fraleigh 2005: 327).

Hijikata and Ohno, studied with proponents of German Expressionism – as expressionist creativity probing a collective unconscious spread to Japan and other countries. Dalcroze Technique and German *Neue Tanz* were imported to Japan through Yamada Kosaku and sustained in the influential teaching of Ishii Baku. Eguchi Takaya who studied with Mary Wigman imported the creative experiments and developmental physical techniques of *Neue Tanz*. Eguchi's teaching spread two ways in Japan: toward the growth of lyric and dramatic modern dance through such contemporary artists as Kanai Fumie (who became his assistant), and also toward the more gestural and raw dance of butoh through Ohno and Hijikata. Ohno studied with Ishii in 1933 and Eguchi in 1936, and Hijikata first studied German-style modern dance as a young man in rural Akita under Masumura Katsuko, a student of Eguchi. Later he studied with Ando Mitsuko a disciple of Eguchi. Ohno and Hijikata met through Ando sometime between 1952 and 1954. Ohno's six page vita and biography notes his experience of seeing expressionist Harald Kreutzberg, a student of Wigman, dance in 1934; this inspired him to study with Eguchi and his wife, Miya Misako, who had studied with Wigman and returned to Japan to teach the new German dance.

Cultural assimilation was not a one-way street, however. Before Japanese dancers began to study the emerging modern dance abroad, the expressively stylized and much admired Japanese Ukiyo-e woodblock color prints were popular in America and Germany. Aesthetic exchange between Japan and the West developed from world trade and travel after Japan opened its doors to foreigners in 1868 at the end of the *Edo* period and fifteen generations of Tokugawa Shoguns during this period from about 1615 to 1868. *Edo* is the original name for modern Tokyo, and it also designates a period in Japan's history that brought peace – an end of internecine warfare and a flourishing of the arts under the authority of the shoguns. As the economic power of the bourgeoisie grew, it undermined the shogunate's artistic hegemony, leading to a sharing of cultural values and pluralism in the arts that transcended class in shaping a national identity (Guth 1996: 1–11, 168).

Ukiyo-e color prints, originating in the latter half of the seventeenth century and developing throughout the *Edo* period, had become wildly fashionable in Europe and the United States by the late nineteenth century and in the early twentieth century. Scholars and collectors became connoisseurs. The French impressionists Edouard Manet, Edgar Degas, Henri de Toulouse-Lautrec, Paul Gauguin, and American Mary Cassat shared an admiration of the Ukiyo-e woodcuts (Ives 1974). Ukiyo-e included depictions of the "rough stuff" or dynamic *aragoto* acting style of the early Kabuki Theater that audiences in *Edo* found so appealing. Long before the emergence of stylized emotional dancing in German expressionism and butoh, Ukiyo-e displayed distorted and ferocious dancing figures in a kind of *aragoto* dance theater painting if you will. Ukiyo-e artist Torii Kiyonobu who began working in *Edo* in 1687 developed a stereotypical figural style depicting rough style *aragoto* actor-dancers with "legs shaped like inverted gourds and wriggling-worm contours" (Guth 1996: 100). Butoh, likewise, cultivates stooped and bow-legged postures, wild sweeps of movement, and wriggling contours. So much so that some of the first Japanese audiences for butoh, even though they could appreciate highly stylized traditional versions of bodily distortions, choreographed awkwardness, wrathful and pathetic figures in the Kabuki Theater, wondered why butoh dancers moved as if "crazy" or "handicapped." A friend of Hijikata's, the poet Yoshioka Minoru, wrote that Hijikata's inspiration for the 1972 series known as "Tohoku Kabuki," *Shiki no tame no nijushichiban*, came from *Nishiki-e*, multi-colored Ukiyo-e (Yoshioka 1987: 56–7).

Early expressionism in Germany also stylized raw expression and frenzied emotion, especially Wigman's *Witch Dance* of 1926, springing from features of Japanese and Javanese cultures. Wigman has described how easy it was to throw herself into fits of emotion in her improvisational work with Rudolph von Laban and in preparing her dances. At the same time, she emphasized the bond between form and expression in classes that Sondra Fraleigh took with her from 1965 through 1966. Wigman, a key teacher of early pioneers in Japanese modern dance, was herself influenced by Eastern aesthetics. Ernst Scheyer writes that in Dresden in the middle twenties Wigman's interest in the East was reinforced by her contact with the Dresden Ethnological Museum and with Felix Tikotin who exhibited his full collection of Oriental art in the Gallery Arnold in 1923. Victor Magito, a mask carver who had experimented with Japanese Noh masks, created the mask for Wigman's *Ceremonial Figure* in 1925 (Scheyer 1970: 20). Dance in the United States during the first decade of the twentieth century also incorporated the East — often through trite Oriental imitations in ballet, the interpretive dance of the Denishawn School, and Delsarte Orientalism. The dance world seemed intoxicated with exotic and Oriental stereotypes, especially the Ballets Russes.

Now, with butoh's international proliferation and renewals of expressionism through Pina Bausch and others, the expressionist origins of modern dance, once repressed by the American postmodern dance of the 1960s and the objective dance of Merce Cunningham, returns, but with a difference. Butoh presents special challenges in this regard. It is very expressive, but in a unique postmodern way. "The Hanging Body" (Laage 1993) with the dead weight of the head or limbs hanging from taut points of focus in the dancing gesture, and ghostly figures in surrealist costumes, white powder, gothic painting, or mixed message dressing, are aesthetic signatures in butoh. Cross-gender dressing, cross-cultural dressing, and use of music from around the globe attest butoh's postmodern eclecticism and East–West amalgamations.

Butoh dancers contrast these external complications with simple gestures of striving and longing, or minimize theatrical show with diminutive kinaesthetic awakenings that grow and quickly fade before maturing. Butoh techniques include blunt and wild motifs thrown into space, like Waguri Yukio's, or rhythmic gyrations of the torso that flail through the limbs, like Mikami Kayo's. At the other extreme, dancers may pause suddenly in silence and shift to embryonic floating, like Ohno Kazuo, or develop eternally slow and grounded walking, falling down lightly without making a sound, seeming empty, like Ashikawa Yoko. At times dancers like Kasai Akira incorporate technical dance movement from other forms. His butoh includes inspiration from the dance of Isadora Duncan and Mary Wigman, and he also uses eurythmy, a dance like form of body training founded by the mystic philosopher Rudolph Steiner in 1921 that he studied in Germany in 1979. Some current butoh dancers like Yamada Setsuko even incorporate the sheer lightness of ballet and the sculpting of modern dance in their butoh, blending these with the lowered center of gravity found in tai chi. (Fraleigh 1999 provides full descriptions of the works of the foregoing artists.) Indeed, butoh draws the witness into an emotional space through its reach into the dark soul. Still more, through its ability to transform negatives into positives, it empties a place in the mind for spiritual recognition. Butoh has an improvisatory basis, but it also cultivates structured choreography with a significant change from early expressionism. Ohno Kazuo states the difference: "As long as the body maintains an existence marked by social experience, it cannot express the soul with purity" (Viala and Sekine 1988: 94). Like characters in calligraphy, butoh characters are signs and transparencies. The butoh dancer's manner of shedding the social body is immediate.

Life in a speck of dust, dance in a drop of sweat: butoh has taken surprising directions. *I-ki*, Yoshioka Yumiko's butoh installation of 2003 in collaboration with Joachim Manger, is a daredevil escape from a labyrinth of plastic tubes. Wet with the sweat of dare, the dancer makes her way through the plastic, barely breathing, carrying a knife in her pocket (just in case): danger, dance, or game of suffocation? Yoshioka bases her work in Germany and performs in Europe, Canada, and the United States. Non-Japanese butoh artists also perform internationally. These include Su-En, aka Susanna Akerlund from Sweden who was given her butoh name by her teacher Ashikawa Yoko, and Ledoh, a dancer from Burma with his butoh company *Salt Farm* based in San Francisco. Circling back to Hijikata's influence, *Harupin-ha*, a dance company in Berkeley California formed by Tamano Koichi and his wife, Hiroko, has performed on world tours with the popular contemporary musician Kitaro. In Japan, Tamano's teacher Hijikata anointed him the "bow-legged Nijinsky." Recent Japanese butohists who perform internationally and hark back to Hijikata and Ohno for their inspiration are Katsura Kan, Endo Tadashi, and the all female company of Kawamoto Yuko.

HIJIKATA: A CORPSE STANDING DESPERATELY UPRIGHT

Hijikata grew up in rural Tohoku in the rustic Akita prefecture of the northern region of Japan's main island of Honshu. He died of liver disease at the age of fifty-seven, having dedicated his life to dance. He had created not only a new form of dance, but also a wide circle of artistic associates with whom he enjoyed a lively social life, and he had inspired a generation of students who remained fiercely dedicated to him. Hijikata first became exposed to Western culture at age eighteen when he began studying *Neue Tanz*, the German dance movement that began early in the twentieth century with the work of Laban and Wigman among others. Eventually, he came into contact with Western surrealist literature and poetry and the techniques of classical ballet. Through his discontent with ballet, he began to search for his own style of expression. Mikami Kayo writes that Hijikata's development as an artist through modernization provides a prototype for the discontent of modern Japanese artists since the Meiji restoration of 1868, and the growing encroachment of Western values. She sees that Japanese artists have experienced two stages since then, first turning to the West for new models, then facing East, looking back into their own identity (1993: 38–40). In this regard Hijikata was no exception. He followed in the wake of many Japanese artists after the *Meiji* period, but an ancestral path marked his search for originality. Looking back, Hijikata embodied the pain of his childhood and connected with his Japanese heritage.

Japan was forced into the modern era in 1853 when Admiral Commodore Mathew C. Perry of the American Navy sailed into Tokyo's harbor and ordered Japan open to commerce (as noted in the introduction). The *Meiji* era began in 1868 with Japan's new relationship to the world outside. Since 1945 and Japan's defeat by the United States in World War II, Westernization had accelerated. It reached a high point in the 1960s. This was also a time of struggle over the renewal of the US–Japan Security Treaty forged at the end of the war. Inevitably, the ways of the West were questioned in Japan. In the fields of theater and dance, artists sought to rescue the Japanese body from Western dualism. The Western effacement of the Japanese body is examined brilliantly by Noguchi Hiroyuki (2004) in 'The Idea of the Body in Japanese Culture and its Dismantlement'. It was in the 1960s that Hijikata reached a turning point; he questioned the West's logic, its split of body and spirit in refusal of the flesh. Thus his seminal work – *Revolt of the Flesh* (1968) – initialing *Ankoku Butoh* – darkness dance.

YONEYAMA KUNIO

Hijikata Tatsumi (born Yoneyama Kunio) was the sixth son and tenth child of eleven. His parents were farmers and owned a buckwheat noodle (*soba*) shop. Hijikata himself pointed out the relationship between his birthplace of Akita and *Ankoku Butoh* – his dance of utter darkness. In his speech '*Kaze Daruma*' (1985), he describes a link between butoh's signature physiology, shrinking arms and legs, and the physicality of people in the country. The folded-up legs of infants kept in rice preservers, Hijikata said, inspired his butoh. He used features such as bowlegs and muddy feet in rice fields to teach the physicality of butoh, which contrasts with the verticality of Western dance, and he created improvisational processes like the "Mold-Ambulation" and "Bug-Ambulation" from his memories of rural life. Butoh teacher and performer Yoshioka Yumiko believes Hijikata used his sense of place as a universal metaphor: "There is a Tohoku in England," he said, and "Northeast is everywhere" (Yoshioka, Interview in Fraleigh 1999: 245–6).

He also based his public image on his poor-farmer family background, but his father was in fact the son of a village mayor, and Hijikata sometimes wore Western clothes. While fortunate in some ways, he nevertheless writes in a 1969 article, 'From Being Jealous of a Dog's Vein', of childhood terrors and endless days of soggy rice crackers. No doubt the poverty surrounding Hijikata in pre-war Tohoku shaped his early development; as he often complained: "What Tohoku exports are horses, women, soldiers, and rice." In his '*Kaze Daruma*' speech of 1985, he talks of the disturbing feelings and movements of three-year-old babies as he observes them tied to posts and left alone in their farmhouses. They probably felt themselves to be *other* he says: "Their bodies were not their own. . . . What I learned from those toddlers has greatly influenced my body." He also speculates about the limitations of his own body as he speaks of babies placed in *izume*, a rice-warming basket, while their parents worked in the rice paddies. The children were tied down and "bawled endlessly" as Hijikata remembers: "In the damp open sky a gluttonous wind swallows the children's screams" (2000d: 74–78). Hijikata reflects on human symbiosis and remembrance of place. But we should also notice that his Tohoku is emblematic, a primal landscape of Japan that is now lost.

STUDYING *NEUE TANZ*

In 1945 at the age of seventeen, Hijikata graduated from Akita Prefecture Technical High School and went to work for the Akita Steel Company. The next year he started taking lessons in *Neue Tanz*, the German modern dance movement, at the Masumura Katsuko Dance School in the lineage of Eguchi Takaya. (Eguchi and his wife Miya Misako, both from Tohoku region, studied with Wigman from 1931 to 1933, and returned as influential teachers of *Neue Tanz*.) Hijikata toured rural farming villages with his first teacher, Masumura, and eventually wrote in a 1960 article, 'Inner Material/Material', about the circumstances of his first dance studies:

> I became a disciple of a woman dance teacher in my hometown. I was fond of the phrase 'to become a disciple,' so I put on new underpants and went through the gate to the teacher's house. Because the term 'foreign dance,' however, makes me vaguely anxious, I hesitantly asked her what kind it was, while at the same time thinking I would just quit if it were not what I wanted. When she told me it was German dance, I immediately took steps to become a disciple. I figured that since Germany was hard, its dance too would be hard.
>
> (2000a: 36)

Hijikata was considerably affected by seeing the Hitler *Jugend* (Youth) marching during a tour of Japan. He found the blond boys in uniforms impressive, and feared his female schoolmates might be kidnapped by those grand and orderly young boys. Butoh scholar Kurihara Nanako says Hijikata gained the impression that "things German were impenetrable." She believes this contributed to his notion of male beauty as "a phallic fortress – stark, invincible, immediate, tense, stiff, bare, impenetrable, clear-cut, and acute" (Kurihara 1996: 61). Here we sense the climate of the pre-war military aesthetic in Japan and Europe seen in marching. It is all the more interesting then that as Hijikata's work developed his dancers moved so minimally. "They seemed rather to be protecting something vulnerable inside rather than attacking outward," Kurihara says. She reports that Hijikata desired to make his dancer into a "dreaming murder weapon" (Ibid.). His butoh eventually developed the tough militant outside or yang qualities of phallic male eroticism, countering this with a vulnerable liquid *yin* essence on the inside, leaving an eerie impression unlike anything seen in modern dance, except perhaps the controlled frenzy of Wigman's *Hexentanz* (Witch Dance 1926).

Wearing a mask of her own face made by Japanese Noh mask maker Victor Magito, Wigman sat and turned in a hunched-over minimal pattern, pounding the floor percussively with her feet, while her hands morphed from tense claws to delicate flutters grazing the still mask. Modern dance grew throughout the twentieth century as a discovery form of dance focusing on creative and personal resources in contrast to the stylizations of classical ballet. Ishii, Eguchi, and others who studied in Europe and America in the second and third decades of the twentieth century introduced it to Japan, as we saw. The mainstream modern dance in Japan before World War II was German Expressionism, or *Neue Tanz*: Sometimes termed "Poison Dance" because of its expressive extremes and inclusion of grotesque gestures. The liberating essence of this new dance sparked Hijikata's originality; admitting his body and pushing extremes, he overturned previous styles. In a country where community takes precedence over the individual, his breakthrough inventiveness is all the more amazing.

THE DRUG OF OHNO

During a visit to Tokyo in 1948–1949, the twenty-one-year-old Hijikata saw a dance recital given by Ohno Kazuo at *Kanda Kodo Kyoritsu* Hall that moved him profoundly. This was after Ohno's return home from nine years as a soldier in World War II, the last two years spent as a prisoner of war in New Guinea. In 'Inner Material/Material', Hijikata recalls his encounter with Ohno who later became his partner in the development of butoh:

> In the fall of 1948 in Tokyo, I saw a wonderful dance performance, overflowing with lyricism, by a man wearing a chemise. Cutting the air again and again with his chin, he made a lasting impression on me. For years this drug dance stayed in my memory. That dance has now been transformed into a deadly poison, and one spoonful of it contains all that is needed to paralyze me.
>
> (2000a: 36)

Ohno, who had studied with modern dancers Eguchi and Ishii early in his life, felt dissatisfied with the established style of dance expression in Japan, and was searching for his own style. He was forty-three by 1949, and just beginning to develop his dance career after the war; Hijikata later named Ohno's dance "Poison Dance."

TOKYO

In 1952, Hijikata moved to Tokyo to study dance at the age of twenty-four. He wanted to be a part of the urban art scene, but was in the beginning just a country boy with a quaint dialect adrift in a large city. In 1953 Hijikata entered the Ando Mitsuko Dance Institute. He and Ohno met through Ando. Under Ohno's influence, Hijikata also acquired various styles of Western dance including Spanish, jazz, and ballroom. He started associating with Tokyo's circle of artists as can be seen from his writing, 'Inner Material/Material'. "Rimbaud" was the password for the club. But romance with the fellows who liked Rimbaud gradually faded, as Hijikata admitted: "We welcomed the misery provided by alcohol. The club went downhill when someone who played with guns joined it" (2000a: 38).

In his early days in Tokyo, Hijikata copied the fashions he saw in Hollywood movies and wore his hair like his hero James Dean. He gradually assimilated city life through his association with artists and writers as well as prostitutes. His survival was difficult on the margins of Tokyo society. Although he is not explicit, his writings (ever difficult to decode) refer to trouble with the police in his early days in Tokyo. (In later life, he would operate a nightclub to make ends meet, where members of his company danced nude, and he once again had occasions to dodge the police.) As his work matured, Hijikata let his hair grow long, and achieved a guru status among his followers.

Hijikata's life in Tokyo in the 1950s revolved first around theater and dance; he also worked in a laundry, as a warehouse keeper and long-shoreman, and at one time he lived in a flophouse. During this time he met a group of artists who would later become prominent figures of modern Japanese art – Kawara On, Shinohara Ushio, and the set designer Kanamori Kaoru. He spent time drinking sake with them, and talking about art and theater.

Meanwhile, Motofuji Akiko, an accomplished ballet dancer whom Hijikata later married, established her dance school between 1950 and 1952. This would later become Hijikata's Asbestos-kan (Asbestos Hall theater) school and butoh company. Hijikata's mother died in 1954 the same year that he and Ohno also appeared in their first joint performance *Crow* with the stage artist Okamoto Taro and choreography by Ando, their modern dance teacher.

NEW NAMES

In 1958, a year before his first radical butoh, *Kinjiki* (1959), Yoneyama Kunio took the stage name of Hijikata Tatsumi. A year after this performance, Hijikata began to further formulate his subversive view of dance. His idea for his first recital DANCE EXPERIENCE *no kai* in July of 1960 arose when he realized that he could not accomplish his own dance in the image of the West. The works on this recital included *Hanatachi* (Flowers), *Shorijo* (Disposal Place), *Shushi* (Seeds,) and *Diviinu sho* (Divine), which was a solo for Ohno Kazuo.

While associating with male prostitutes in Ueno-Kurumazaka, Hijikata came up with the idea expressed in 'Inner Material' that he would have to make dances from the material at hand: "I even dreamed of a dance about hair that as a matter of course examines a skinny belly." He thought seriously about "the art of impotence," he says in the same passage, "when a general image of life hit me with unbearable speed. . . . I was completely impotent. All my seeds were cut off. That was when the springs in my legs weakened in the 'dance of sterilization.' Swaying legs are now a technique of my dance. Violence of course had to hit me from without." (Hijikata 2000a: 39). One has the impression of layers upon layers in Hijikata's development of butoh. He finally rejects the "Tokyo spirit" which places the artist above everyone else under the name of art – a spirit without wound or bleeding. Against arts of capitalist production and the "Tokyo spirit," Hijikata casts his "Imitation Arts," "Impotent Arts," and "Terror Dance."

He married Motofuji in 1968 and took her last name, changing his legal name to Motofuji Kunio. This was the same year that he choreographed his signature work *Revolt of the Flesh* as harbinger to *Ankoku Butoh*. His last performance before beginning to choreograph extensively for others was *Summer Storm* in 1973; by then his work had matured considerably and he had established his dance company. In October of 1974, he choreographed *Ankoku butoh ebisuya ocho* (The Utter Darkness butoh Ocho at House of Ebisu) for the formal opening of Asbestos Hall Theater, named in dubious honor of Motofuji's father, whose business was selling asbestos (another kind of poison). *Ankoku* was taken from popular French movies at the time – the "film noir," which is *Ankoku Eiga* (Black Film) in Japanese. Hijikata named his new form of dance *Ankoku Butoh*.

Motofuji and Hijikata had two daughters; eventually she gave up her career to support his work and take care of their children, and in later years, she managed his nightclub. More recently, until her death in 2003, she and Hijikata's daughters oversaw the archives dedicated to his life and work. Meanwhile, she also became a butoh training master and officially the managing director of the Hijikata Tatsumi Memorial Asbestos Studio. It is increasingly clear that Motofuji is one of butoh's unsung heroes, initiating the endeavors of butoh with Hijikata, and also explaining them through her book *Together with Hijikata Tatsumi (Hijikata Tatsumi to tomo ni)* (1990). Among Hijikata and Motofuji's early dances together are *Roses for Emily* and *Aerial Garden*. After his death, she choreographed *Mandara* (1993), *A letter to Abakanowicz* (1994), and *Heaven: We Walk on Eternity* (1997), combining butoh innovatively with ballet and *Neue Tanz* in a sweeping style of expression. Motofuji also directed *Theoria of Mirrors* in 1997 and performed together with Ohno Kazuo and Yoshito for the first time in thirty years, furthering possibilities of the butoh form. At her death, dancers held a memorial performance in honor of Motofuji.

DANCING LIFE: OHNO KAZUO

A fetus walked along a snow-covered path. It cleared a path by spreading its clothes upon the snow after removing them one by one as in a secret cosmic ceremony. Then it peeled off its skin and laid that upon the path. A whirlwind of snow surrounded it, but the fetus continued, wrapped in this whirlwind. The white bones danced, enveloped by an immaculate cloak. This dance of the fetus, which moved along as if carried by the whirlwind of snow, seemed to be transparent.

(Ohno Kazuo in Holborn 1987: 36)

As aesthetic associates, Hijikata and Ohno represent two opposites of a yin/yang magnetic polarity. While Hijikata celebrates the negative in his themes of death and sacrifice, in ugly beauty, and in mud, Ohno also spirals downward, but with a fluid spirituality. For Ohno, the sacred is dynamic and organic, belonging to the embryo in the mother's womb, and to the dance, just as his classes often revolve around spiritual matters. Ohno was already a mature and skillful modern dancer when the young Hijikata saw him dance in a dress to lyrical poetry by the German poet Rilke: "flower, flower let's bloom – in the summer there will be a great harvest" (Ohno and Ohno 2004: 181). This would have been the first of five modern dance recitals Ohno performed in Tokyo between 1949 and 1959 (Chronology of Public Appearances, Ohno and Ohno 2004: 315). (Hijikata remembers the performance as 1948 in 'Inner Material/Material'.)

Ohno was born in Hakodate City, Hokkaido, in 1906. Upon gradua-tion from the Japan Athletic College, he began working as a physical education teacher at *Kanto Gakuin* High School, a private Christian school for girls in Yokohama. After seeing a performance in 1928 by the Spanish dancer Antonia Mercé known as La Argentina, he was so impressed that he decided to dedicate his life to dance. He began training with two of Japan's modern dance pioneers, Ishii Baku and Eguchi Takaya. His interest in this period was in modern expressionist dance. Ohno's conversion to Christianity was a major influence in his life and on his dances with their recurring themes of life, death, and rebirth. Even before being drafted into the military, he converted to and became a follower of the Baptist faith influenced by Sakata Tasuke, the principal of *Kanto Gakuin* High School where he first taught (Ohno and Ohno 2004: 112–114). "When I became a Christian in 1930," he says, "I expected some significant change in my life, but nothing happened. It takes time to understand and incarnate an idea." Ohno appears to have thought deeply into Christian issues, for instance the concept of judg-ment: "I have thought, why did Judas hang himself even though he was forgiven?" (Slater 1986: 7–8).

Equally important were his beliefs as a non-church pacifist, nearly a decade of experiences in World War II, and the influence of his mother and other defining women in his life. Such motivating forces were por-trayed in his dances – *Jellyfish Dance* (1949), *Admiring La Argentina* (1977), and *My Mother* (1981). Ohno's accounts of the war are fragmented, but this is what we do know. In 1938 he was called up for military service and spent the following nine years in active service in China and New Guinea; his final two years in the military were spent as a prisoner of war in the jungles of New Guinea. Out of eight thousand prisoners he was among the two thousand few who survived. Ohno rarely talks about the war, except when he speaks generally in his workshops about how "many people die in wars to serve the living," and that we who survive carry the dead within our bodies. For himself, he says: "I carry all the dead with me" (Fraleigh 1999: 57). Yoshito feels his father's experiences as a soldier must have been horrifying, and he thinks that Ohno "talks" about his experiences through his dances. *Jellyfish Dance* in 1949, his first public performance after returning home in 1946, is thought to depict

Figure 1.4 Ohno Kazuo in military uniform, circa 1938. Courtesy Ohno Kazuo
    Archive

the burials at sea he witnessed on the crowded ship carrying repatriated prisoners of war home to Japan (Ohno and Ohno 2004: 85, 110).

Yoshito provides us with an account of his father through the eyes of a son who practiced and danced with him from a young age, first performing under his father's watchful eye in Hijikata's very controversial *Kinjiki* when he was just twenty. In a video production of Ohno's life, *96 Years Old: Lifelong Butohist, Dancing in My Hometown*, one sees the complete dedication and respect that Yoshito has toward his father in his old age, and how he so tenderly takes care of him (ETV 2003). Ohno gets constant attention and love from his wife and family, especially his son and dancing partner, and he continues to participate in dance by being present in the classes that Yoshito teaches in their now famous Yokohama studio carrying on his father's work. Students acknowledge Ohno as they bask in his presence, and sometimes he performs for them in his wheelchair. Ohno is seen performing in *Hakodate tokubetsu koen: Waga haha no oshie tamaishi uta* (Special Performance in Hakodate: The Song My Mother Taught Me); Yoshito wheels him up the aisle where a full house greets him, then onto the stage where he continues to live through the sensitive gestures of his spontaneous dance. Audiences are certainly aware that Ohno will reach his 100th birthday in 2006, and they celebrate every movement as golden.

Ohno and Yoshito have been father-son dance partners for over forty years. Their first joint performance was in *The Old Man and the Sea* in 1959 at Ohno's fifth recital. They complement each other in this work, as the younger Ohno's minimal slow movement diagonally across the stage grounds the space–time frame of the scene, while the older Ohno flies around in waltzes and expressive gestures processing body–time. This is the same partnering technique still used in *Suiren* (Water Lilies) in 1987. Ohno bases this dance on Monet's painting of the same name with Yoshito appearing as a tense, blocky masculine figure in the first scene, against his father's soft delicate dance with a parasol, both figures in transit to later images as Yoshito becomes the lily (the lotus goddess) and Ohno mimes and dances freely in a black suit. The audience senses a mutual respect and symbiosis between them. Yoshito – an unassuming butoh hero from the very beginning – is a constant assistant and collaborator in the work of his father and Hijikata.

Ohno's life is dance and performance. In his quiet way, he is always "on." Yoshito says that the father he knows on stage is more of a real father than in day-to-day life, showing great love and emotion that he

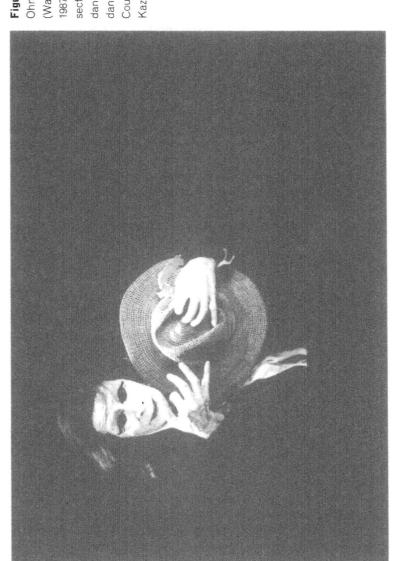

Figure 1.5
Ohno in *Suiren* (Water Lilies, 1987). In the last section of the dance, Ohno dances freely. Courtesy Ohno Kazuo Archive

rarely expresses openly when not performing. His dances in the early years before collaboration with Hijikata were about life (*sei*), expressing the feeling of someone who is full of life. "Life comes from the mother," Ohno says in his workshops: "Go back to the womb and feel how your embryo self moves" (Ohno in Fraleigh 2004: 255). For Ohno, dance takes shape only if there is spiritual content, and form is a flowing expression of body that projects "the inner voice" (Ohno and Ohno 2004: 18). Ohno's very expressive face and extremely large hands rivet audiences. His inner world unfolds through an expressive use of the mouth, what he thinks of as "the eyes of the body," the listening ears of the soul, and even the back of the body felt by the audience – as we see in a chapter of Yoshito's book that describes his father's dance methods (Ohno and Ohno 2004: 9–40). Bearing humanity with him, Ohno falls off his feet into another boundless world that takes the audience beyond the floor to a limitless universe (Ohno and Ohno 2004: 41).

BORN TO DANCE

I simply received all things that moved me as they were, and I try to pass them to you.

(Ohno Kazuo in Slater 1986: 7)

Hijikata's anti-social courage gave birth to the theater dance movement that he called Ankoku Butoh. However, it was Hijikata and Ohno's interactive collaborations that projected butoh into a living dance genre. Hijikata admired Ohno, and even when directing Ohno's dances treated him with fatherly respect. Ohno's theater performances, never simply for show, were always genuine, as thousands experienced through his international tours. One day, at the apartment of dancers Eiko and Koma in New York City, he responded to Richard Schechner's question about how he cools down after a particularly moving performance:

Ohno: Me, I never cool down. A good performance is like going to a doctor and getting good medicine. I feel great.
Koma: Actually, I think he is always excited like this.
Ohno: At the age of nearly 80, there is no more "stage" and "daily life."
Eiko: He doesn't commute.

(Schechner 1986: 169)

In being himself, albeit through the guise of amazing theatricality, Ohno often leaves audiences in tears. His extraordinary physical gifts and gentle mind, as also his childlike innocence in improvisation, move them deeply. Gestating over long periods and appealing to multinational audiences, his panoramic dances are never arbitrary. Ohno carried his vision of the flamenco dancer La Argentina with him for fifty years before he danced in her memory. The vision returned, he said, now and again: "But no matter if I called her or cried for her, she never appeared in front of me again, though she hid deep in my soul" (Ohno in Holborn 1987: 38). Hijikata carried his dead sister inside his body: A Flamenco dancer possessed Ohno. What a pair!

Ohno was born to dance, and also a superb actor, able to excavate great depths of emotion through his agile body and compassionate facial expressions. On the historical world stage, he can be compared with Isadora Duncan through the generous spirit of his dance and his power to move audiences. In *Suiren* (Water Lilies), there is a sense of pathos that follows in the wake of Ohno's motions, traces of body memory as he trades his body for ours, dancing sometimes as an old woman, and at others like a lithe Fred Astaire (without the taps). Ohno doesn't show emotion nearly so much as he becomes it, with pain and love pervading every gesture, no matter what the theme of the dance.

Yoshito says that when his father isn't dancing he gets bored, but let someone ask him to dance, or even mention it, and Ohno comes to life. Likewise as a teacher in his studio in Yokohama, Ohno is alive to the moment, mischievous sometimes, and a chameleon; he is butoh morphology personified. But Ohno is more than butoh; he is himself, always. This is clear in his approach to dance when he speaks of his work *Admiring La Argentina*, voicing his admiration for the real Argentina:

> The dance of La Argentina invited people to a sea of excitement. She embodied dance, literature, music, and art, and furthermore she represented love and pain in real life. She would have said, 'It was not my art that moved people. I simply received all things that moved me as they were, and I try to pass them to you. I am simply a servant conveying these things to you'.
>
> (Ohno in Holborn 1987: 38)

The very sensitive Ohno, a Christian pacifist, experienced serious pain through his forced participation in the war. Hijikata recognized something of this in Ohno when he saw him dance, sensing his connection with an inner resource he himself was trying to release, though perhaps not so transparently as Ohno. Like the Greek satyrs and comic actors with their harnessed-on exaggerated *phalloi* (Cahill 2003: 130, 134, 209), Hijikata, an enormous bronzed erection strapped to his body, belongs to the word of form; Ohno, who can break your heart with longing and hope for an unseen presence, belongs to the world of spirit. He and Hijikata eventually develop divergent philosophies of form in dance. Hijikata believes that "life catches up with form" so that when there is structure, content will naturally follow. Ohno, however, feels that "form comes by itself," if initially there is spiritual content (Ohno and Ohno 2004: 94). In his workshop words he says:

> Spirit comes first when you dance. When you walk, do you think about your feet? There isn't anyone who thinks about their feet. When a mother calls to her child, 'Come here,' the child responds, 'Mother.' Life is always like that. It doesn't remain still.
>
> (Ohno 1997: 83)

To cast the chemistry of their partnership widely from East to West: Ohno, "the poison dancer" by Hijikata's account, delivers "the scorpion sting," an image that pre-Socratic Greek philosopher Heraclitus uses for moments of recognition that break through the universal continuum of time. Ohno's acute expression of life is a "wake up call" that peaks Hijikata's desire to arrest the forms of his pain. In an interview with Susan Klein, Ohno said that he and Hijikata had personalities on opposite ends of the spectrum (Klein 1988: 6). The polarized extremes of Ohno and Hijikata released the stunning energy that produced the original *Ankoku Butoh*.

TOGETHER AND APART

Just prior to their 1960–1968 period of close collaboration in creating DANCE EXPERIENCE, both Hijikata and Ohno appeared in *Crow* choreographed by Ando at the Ando Mitsuko Dance Institute. It was 1954 and Hijikata's first public performance in Tokyo. Hijikata later served as stage director for Ohno's Fifth Modern Dance Recital in 1959. Ohno was attracted to Hijikata's experimental approach to dance. After Hijikata and Ohno started working closely together, Ohno's dance radically changed. His dances had been full of life (*sei*) but soon he began reflecting on the question of death (*shi*), which became the focus for his creative process. *Shi to sei* (death and life) become the two prominent themes around which Ohno's performances evolve. In 1960, just one year after his first work *Kinjiki*, Hijikata choreographs *Diviinu sho* (Divine) for Ohno, a solo inspired by Divine the hero/ine of Genet's novel *Our Lady of the Flowers*. In the opening scene of *Divine* (Divine's Death), Ohno portrays the dying moments of an elderly male prostitute. In the second scene, "Rebirth as a Young Girl," a different person is born in the place where the prostitute died. Ohno recalls his early collaborative encounters with Hijikata as the time he came face to face with his soul, dancing *Divine*:

> This was my first encounter with Genet, my encounter with Hijikata, my encounter with myself. My dance encounter is with Mankind, an encounter with Life.
>
> (Ohno in Viala and Sekine 1988: 26)

The production of *Divine* marked the beginning of an intense working relationship between Ohno and Hijikata that lasted eight years. Then they parted company for about ten years from 1968 until 1977 when Hijikata again directed Ohno, this time in the performance of *Admiring La Argentina*, one of Ohno's signature works. Yoshito says the hiatus was not out of animosity, and that their work together naturally came to a close in this phase. Each of them went through a period of inner reflection. Hijikata's *Ankoku butoh-ha* group performed for the last time in 1966. Then he undertook a three-year groundbreaking project with photographer Hosoe Eikoh. Returning home to look for their common roots in Tohoku, Hijikata and Hosoe sought to capture the spirit of the *kamaitachi*, literally sickle-weasel, also referring to a cut on the skin caused by a mythical whirlwind that creates a vacuum of air. In this sharp illusive animal image, the photographer conjures the wounded dancer/ magician of a forgotten past, seen not on stage but by local witnesses as a phantom flashing by. Hosoe, who had lived in northern Tohoku as a child, won the 1970 Ministry of Education Arts Encouragement Prize for *Kamaitachi* (1969), his book of photographs of Hijikata, immortalizing butoh in compelling outdoor portraits of the dancer in the rustic fields Tohoku. Since the late 1990s, Hosoe has been working on a book of photographs of Ohno.

Ohno went through an identity crisis filled with self-searching during this hiatus and could not perform in front of an audience. He starred in a series of films directed by Nagano Chiaki, called *The Trilogy of Mr O*: "The Portrait of Mr O" (1969), "Mandala of Mr O" (1971) and "Mr O's Book of the Dead" (1973). "Mandala of Mr O" echoes Ohno's voyage of self-discovery. The emotional turmoil in these films proved cathartic. Fascinated by such things as pig squalor and filth, Ohno incorporated the ugly underbelly of beauty in Nagano's films, thinking nothing of falling to the ground and sucking a sow's teat. He may never have gone back to dancing if he had not had time for exploration, synthesis, and healing. In a chance visit to an art gallery, he saw an abstract painting of geometrical curves painted on a zinc sheet by Nakanishi Natsuyuki that inspired him to make a dance dedicated to Mercé Antonia – a Spanish dancer born in 1890 in Buenos Aires and known as La Argentina. As a young man of about twenty-three, Ohno saw her dance at the Imperial Theater in Tokyo. "I could feel her presence," Ohno said on remembering her through the painting, "I could see her there dancing among those flowing curves." This inspiration brought him back to the stage in an intimate autobiographical dance, connecting his own life to Argentina's through the music of Ikeda Mitsuo's seven-member tango orchestra. (The tango was also one of the favored rhythms of *Neue Tanz*; Ohno had performed this Latin form in his studies with Miya and Eguchi who popularized the tango in Japan.) He dedicated his comeback performance to La Argentina's memory in *Admiring La Argentina* (1977). On a visit in 1980 to her grave in Neuilly, a suburb of Paris, Ohno wept and realized "the price she paid to live." He clung to her tombstone he says, "not wanting to leave her . . . ever" (*Admiring La Argentina* program notes, trans. Barrett, 1988).

TOGETHER AGAIN

Beginning with Hijikata's direction of *Admiring La Argentina*, Ohno became an even greater dancer in the decade in which he and Hijikata reconnected. The renaissance that Ohno experienced in his early seventies blossomed into a collaboration with Hijikata from 1977 to 1986 in which they choreographed dances that could be recreated on stage. This was a shift from their former experimental "Dance Experiences" (as they called them) that were ephemeral one-time performances created in the moment. Most of the dances that became part of Ohno's repertoire were from this late period of collaboration – with the younger Hijikata as director and the elder Ohno as dancer. Ohno sometimes spoke of his attraction to Hijikata's dance methods: "The most important thing that I received from Mr. Hijikata was the power and strength of eroticism; he could show that it was so exquisite, something so strong that people were afraid of it" (Ohno in Slater 1986: 8).

In his working relationship with Hijikata, Ohno also encountered death again, not so literally as he had in war, but in the dances of death that Hijikata created. It is far from surprising then that in Ohno's return to the stage after almost a decade of self-reflection he would choose once again to collaborate with the man who had brought him face to face with himself. Their dance, *The Dead Sea*, premiered at the *Tokyo Butoh Festival* in February 1985, and was to be the last collaboration of Ohno, Yoshito, and Hijikata. This was also the occasion of Hijikata's famous speech *Kaze Daruma*, declaring the childhood source of his butoh in the mud and wind of Tohoku, and just one year before his death.

OHNO'S INTERNATIONAL STAGE

Ohno is butoh's ambassador:

> Butoh's best moment is the moment of extreme weariness when we make a supreme effort to overcome exhaustion. That reminds me of my show in Caracas. I was covered in sweat. My body had grown old and I was working like a rickety old car, but I was happy. Is that what we call wearing oneself out for glory?
>
> (Ohno Kazuo in Slater 1986: 8)

Achieving world renown at the age of seventy-four, a time when most dancers have long since retired, Ohno became the leading international representative of butoh. While the 1985 *Tokyo Butoh Festival* introduced butoh to the mainstream in Japan, Ohno had already introduced it to the world outside. After Ohno premiered his comeback performance, *La Argentina Sho* (Admiring La Argentina) in 1977 in Japan, he performed this same work in 1980 at the *14th International Theatre Festival* in Nancy, France. Even though Sankai Juku and other butoh performers were part of the festival, as primogeniture, Ohno's performance represented butoh's introduction to the world stage. He continued his international tour at this time with performances in Strasbourg, London, Stuttgart, Paris and Stockholm. With Hijikata directing, he created two more major works, *My Mother* (1981) and *The Dead Sea* (1985) performed with Yoshito; both of these dances he subsequently performed abroad. Other repertoire works that follow include *Suiren* (Water Lilies 1987), *Ka Cho Fu Getsu* (Flowers and Birds, Wind and Moon 1990), *Oguri Hangan* (A White Lotus Blossom 1992), and *Terute Hime* (Princess Terute 1992). *Tendo Chido* (The Road in Heaven, The Road in Earth 1995) was initially presented in Indonesia. As one of the most significant international butoh performers, Ohno toured throughout Europe, North and South America, Australia and Asia. Well into old age, Ohno performed in Hong Kong, Korea, Singapore, Taiwan, Indonesia, France, Spain, Denmark, Poland, Canada and the United States.

Ohno's contribution to dance is recognized both in Japan and internationally as evidenced by his many public awards – signaling endeavors that go beyond the original reactive underground movement of butoh. Among his recognitions, Ohno earned the Dance Critic's Circle Award for his acclaimed performance of *La Argentina*, a cultural award from Kanagawa Prefecture in 1993, a cultural award from Yokohama city in 1998, the Michelangelo Antonioni Award for the Arts in 1999, and the Asahi Performing Arts Award in 2002.

OHNO IS A BRIDGE

The body in butoh is already the universe dancing on the borders of life and death.

(Ohno Kazuo with Dopfer and Tangerding (in conversation) 1994: 55)

Ohno's philosophy of dance is grounded in the belief that if we do not go beneath the surface of our everyday lives, then we cannot call what we are doing "dance." His ontological and spiritual concerns grounded in bodily experiences of birth, maturation, and death cross national and cultural boundaries. Such universals are not limited to time and place, even if their representation often is. Ohno embodies the image he dances, not so much symbolizing or representing it. Ever young and old, his body is by now marked and wrinkled by the human affections he communicates. Ohno's stage is the world, and he consciously draws other cultures into himself. His work *The Dead Sea* is inspired by themes of mortality spurred by an on-site visit, relaying his continuing theme of life and death in the mother:

In the stark ecology of the desert there is an absolute relatedness of the rodent to the landscape. The rodent feeds on the dying landscape much like the fetus consumes the nourishment of the mother's body.

(Ohno in McGee 1986: 49)

Because of Ohno's birth in the culturally rich port city of Hakodate, he is acquainted with foreign influences from a very young age. There he encounters the West through the American and British embassies. At home his mother creates an international ambience through her love of Western music, French cooking and literature. As the eldest boy and second child in a family of ten, Ohno, reputedly his mother's favorite, loves to listen to her read aloud the ghost stories of Lafcadio Hearn, a Western resident of Japan and writer of things Japanese in the late 1800s. We also know that Ohno first encounters dance styles through German expressionism and American modern dance. The butoh he finally exports from Japan has incorporated the multicultural scenes of his life, even as his dancing becomes increasingly more layered through his travels abroad. We see this cultural matrix in Ohno's costumes – from masculine tuxedos, to Victorian gowns, and antique Japanese kimonos; as also in one of his favorite encores, he prances to Elvis Presley's songs (or waves his arms to the music from his wheelchair), transporting audiences across time and space – from Japan's premier butohist to America's popular icon.

Ohno's global appeal is beyond the boundaries of race and gender as he assimilates the feminine and the cultural other. He is furthermore a bridge between modern dance and butoh, moving past them in the end. Nakamura Fumiaki (1993), a butoh critic in his conversation with Yoshito, helps us understand Ohno's dance as beyond modern, beyond butoh. Yoshito tells him about a conversation he had with Hijikata:

When Hijikata asked me what I thought of my father's dance, I answered with certainty that his dance is *modaan dansu* (modern dance). Hijikata nodded in total agreement with me. Ohno Kazuo's dance doesn't have to be butoh. His dance cannot be called Japanese aging beauty or *wabi sabi*. Ohno Kazuo has to be lively forever. He has to be *modaan*.

This is not to say that Ohno's dance is within the frame of the existing modern dance, Nakamura cautions. He explains that Ohno has lived through the history of Japanese modern dance represented by Ishii

Baku, Eguchi Takaya and Miya Misako. Ohno's body carries the history of Japanese modern and contemporary dance including the history of butoh. What Yoshito means by *modaan* is a free zone that is beyond the frame of existing dance genres:

What Hijikata Tatsumi saw in Ohno Kazuo's body is *shigen* [natural resource], something he had never seen in any stage art but something he had seen in his own body. Hijikata called what he saw in Ohno Kazuo's body *Ankoku Butoh*.

Hijikata and Yoshito confirm that Ohno embodies the power of life, a vital *shigen* that all dances have internally. *Shigen* is like a vein of gold ore. Of course trinkets can be made from this, and gold can also be orna mental, but the essence that people see in Ohno's dance is pure gold, not artifice (Nakamura 1993: 32–3).

BUTOH, COMMUNITY, AND HEALING

The butoh that Hijikata and Ohno initiated proliferates, often in unpredicted ways, as it is studied and practiced around the globe. Writers focus on the historical, political, and economic conditions that provide the context for the emergence of butoh as a reactionary form (Klein 1988; Kurihara 1996). Butoh performances have been viewed as psychological expression of consciousness through improvisation rather than technical dance (Fisher 1987). Joan Laage, an American butoh dancer and scholar, studied the use and meaning of the body in the theatrical performance of butoh (Laage 1993). Sondra Fraleigh wrote a personal ethnology including accounts of experiences with butoh and Zen in Japan, which includes performance reviews from a philosophical perspective (Fraleigh 1999), and her book *Dancing Identity* examines butoh in context of World War II (Fraleigh 2004). Recent studies by butoh dancers explore butoh as a method of movement therapy (Kasai and Takeuchi 2001), as we take up further in Chapter 4. In an ethnographic and sociological approach, Tamah Nakamura looks at butoh as a context for relationship and community building beyond the performance arena (Nakamura 2006).

Butoh performers have taken their own directions. Takenouchi Atsushi, working in the light of Hijikata and Ohno, but with his own personal stamp, uses nature as an overarching paradigm for his work,

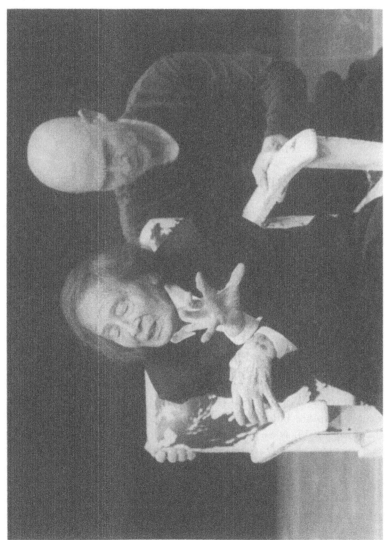

Figure 1.6
Ohno Kazuo
in old age
dances from a
chair with his
son Yoshito
supporting.
Ohno is
"golden,"
Yoshito says:
"he has to be
'Modaan'
(Modern)."
Photograph by
Ikegami Naoya.
Courtesy Ohno
Kazuo Archive

dancing outdoors in every corner of Japan, in Thailand, Cambodia, Europe, and in North and South America, circling the globe. Strongly influenced by Ohno Kazuo, Takenouchi sometimes moves by himself, dancing like a shaman to heal the earth where people have died in great masses. Like many other butoh artists today, he includes elderly people in the fabric of his dances, and especially integrates handicapped people (Takenouchi, Interview with Fraleigh, 2003). The seeds for this inclusiveness were certainly evident in Hijikata and Ohno. The values of communal life have been a butoh hallmark, even if sometimes cultish as with Hijikata and Ashikawa's early efforts to form dance companies in the image of family. Tanaka Min has experimented with communal living also, inviting dancers to live, dance, and work in the Japanese countryside at his *Body Weather Farm* in Hakushu, Yamanashi Prefecture.

The *Seiryukai* dance group in Fukuoka, Japan is establishing a new forum for butoh dancers to build a sustaining, healing community. Harada Nobuo organized Butoh *Seiryukai* in 1994. His former teacher, Kasai Akira, who danced with Hijikata, believes that butoh can heal what he calls "the community body" (Kasai Interview, in Fraleigh, 1999). Kasai sees that butoh can renew the participant and the society through its relational essence. His butoh explorations increase self-awareness and connections between dancers. He teaches that dance can connect us to others and to the past, and that community is more important than individualism. Kasai says that we are not dancing truly if we are not dancing the community body. He reminds us that butoh is dance and not principally an ecological or political movement, but that it also includes all things in nature, not just the human community. The person grows within the community, and through rites that were once the province of magic, can dance toward healing (Ibid.). Harada's concept of "butoh for the people through community building" expands Kasai's view. Harada addresses the social issue of helping young people:

> Most of the young people don't come to dance. They come because they hear about butoh, or see a poster and think it looks different. They come searching for something different. The basic grounding and bonding of human energy used to be expressed through community festivals and other community events in which everyone participated. These events have changed focus so that a few perform while most watch. *Seiryukai* offers a space for a kind of community dance festival.
>
> (Harada Nobuo, Interview with Nakamura, July 6, 2001)

Harada reminds us of the early impetus of butoh, dancing like a shaman in his workshops, inspiring magical transformations with his spirit, and not putting theater performance before the local development of community and dance. He is a good example of what Hijikata talked about when he said he never wanted butoh to become a commercial success. Harada has produced two notable works in this regard, *Hiraku* (Awakening) for children with Down's Syndrome and adults with psychological disorders, and *Keiko no kotoba* (Workshop Words) for the community at large. Developing butoh as therapy, Morita Itto, a butoh performer and practicing psychologist, and Takeuchi Mika, who performs with him, have opened a *Takeuchi Mika Butoh Institute* in Sapporo, Japan that offers butoh classes and stress reduction techniques through their Butoh Dance Therapy Method. In Göttingen, Germany, Endo Tadashi includes people with disabilities in his workshops, mainstreaming them with experienced dancers.

Butoh continues to diversify its means from performance to healing, from the Mexican ritual butoh of Diego Pignon to the evolutionary dance theater of *Sankai Juku*, architecting the pre-history of the body in sandy mystical tones. Probing the dark spot of consciousness, butoh foreshadows wounded healers, shifting shapes in perpetuity: from Hijikata's sacrificial *Ankoku Butoh* to Ohno's haiku poetry in dances that push the boundaries of birth and death. Hijikata's revival of surrealism is marked by profuse imagination, erotic, poetic, and non-rational subject matter, and by resistance to the notion of progress espoused by political and social forces of capitalist democracies. The dance legacy of Hijikata and Ohno is descendant in its general direction. In contrast to Western ballet with its upward ascent, butoh descends to what Hijikata called "the frog's position," drawing up human concerns for the preservation of community in all its diversity, and inspiring personal transformation. Ohno, who makes the whole world his friend, puts the descendant message of butoh this way: "We cannot turn away from the messy refuse of life" (Interview with Fraleigh, 1986).

2

THE WORDS OF
HIJIKATA AND OHNO

This chapter introduces the writings and spoken words of Hijikata and Ohno. We will see how their words relate to their lives and dancing – especially as these two men have highly contrasting characters, and their butoh grows out of this very productive difference.

HIJIKATA-SPEAK

Like whatha, jeez, role dem bones, like the firs'time I got me a dancer, inna sugarcane field it was. body, splap, flung out, shoot me! Like hayhey li'l Jean Genet, damn, I was small too! Wha—t! master Jack O'Bation? Don 'recollect nothin', 'cept dead. . . . sigh—lence sippin' sugarwater when, caught redhanded, man. Whacha doin dancing here for anyway, dumb fuck, course ya get caught,. . . swhat be said.

(Hijikata Tatsumi, spoken monologue 1976
The CoMPaSSioNaTe SouL BiRD comes to unfurl its rustling SKeLeTal WiNGS)

Hijikata's monologue on *Soul Bird* begins with recollections of his childhood and awakening to dance – culminating in his unique Dance Macabre. In a booklet on *Soul Bird*, Matsubara Saika and others describes it as a tour de force, "burning with the ludicrousness of life, which Hijikata's own unique style of Akita accent makes all the more poignant" (Matsubara and others 1998: 6–7). In it we hear the mysterious

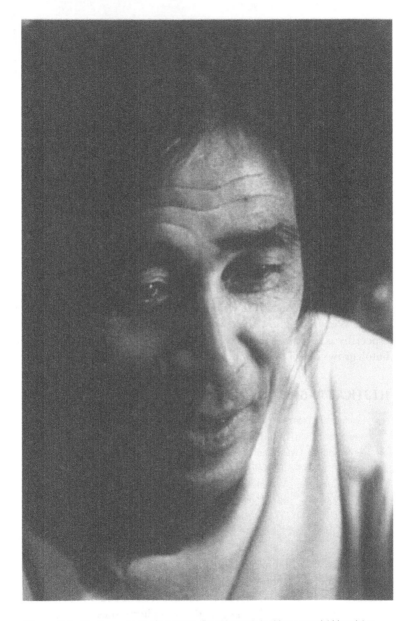

Figure 2.1 Photo portrait of Hijikata. Photograph by Yamaguchi Harahisa. Courtesy Hijikata Tatsumi Archive

unrestricted speech of one who took dance as his ultimate expression. Words seemed to spill from the mouth and dance for Hijikata, like the contemporary patter of rappers.

Similarly, his writings are word paintings, surrealist texts; so non-linear that they prompt a professor of Japanese literature to say, "please translate Hijikata into Japanese." Portions of his writings, however oblique, have been translated into English. Hijikata is a man of many words and dances. His writings are alive with images, embodied nonsequiters, and onomatopoeia, ringing with actions that sound like they feel in the body. Like his dances, raw and unfinished, his writings are somatically derived from the body, and open to interpretation. In a more disjointed manner than James Joyce, he lets go streams of consciousness, and the spoken monologues for which he became famous are even more irrational than his writings.

Hijikata's writing and speaking is consistent with the style of his dances, and when taken as a whole, seem to serve three main purposes. First they seed the reader in the landscape of Tohoku, Hijikata's inspiration for butoh as reinstatement of the folk roots of Kabuki – "Tohoku Kabuki" – as he called it. Secondly, they probe the preconscious shadowy self. We hesitate to call this self "Jungian" because of the Western basis of Carl Jung's theory of the collective unconscious; even though we know Jung's theory is cast inclusively across cultures and histories. Rather there is a more direct route to imagery for Hijikata, not necessarily archetypal as understood in Western terms, but immediately available at the nexus of body and spirit, as we will later explain through Japanese phenomenology of the body. "Inside this one body," Hijikata says, "there are various mythic things that are still sleeping intact. ... The work is how to excavate them at the actual site. ... I would like to see something where such things float up like departed spirits" (Hijikata 'Fragments of Glass' 2000e: 68–9). Lastly, Hijikata's writings serve the purpose of his dances: they both inspire and explain them.

Dance critic Ichikawa Miyabi believes Hijikata repudiates the rule of reason and taming of the body in post-World War II modern dance. His dances and writings are equally seditious, entertaining inexplicable shadows. When Sondra Fraleigh interviewed Ichikawa in Tokyo in 1990, he told her that the unique Japanese love of shadows guided Hijikata's butoh. Japanese novelist Tanizaki Junichiro's *In Praise of Shadows* captures this mellow aspect of Japanese traditions:

I would push back into the shadows the things that come forward too clearly, I would strip away the useless decoration. I do not ask that this be done everywhere, but perhaps we may be allowed at least one mansion where we can turn off the electric lights and see what it is like without them.

(1977: 42)

It was already evident when Tanizaki wrote this in 1933 that the Western tendency toward youth and novelty and its glittering technology were becoming more evident in Japan (Fraleigh 2005: 329).

Although Hijikata is a known master of self-concealment and ambiguity, his language expresses his thoughts directly without editing. For him, capitalist democracy, coming to prominence in Japan after the war, is no more than force, "a Karate technique." It represents a society of production, also turning art into production. He writes: "I am not going to be deceived (by such a Karate movement) anymore." His view of dance as a production is voiced in 'To Prison,' which he wrote in 1961: 'I am a body-shop; my profession is the business of human rehabilitation, which goes today by the name of dancer." Hijikata seeks a purposeless use of the body in a society of productivity. He identifies with homosexuals, festivals, ceremonies, and prisoners because of their lack of purpose in relation to capitalist productivity. "I wager reality on a nonsensical vitality that has purged the echo of logic from my body and I dream of the day when I am sent to prison with them. . . . I would like to be sitting, without even a passport, smack in the middle of a mistake" (2000b: 44–5).

In 'Inner Material/Material' written in 1960, a year after his first work *Kinjiki*, Hijikata carries his protest against production further in terms of performance: "Because audiences pay money to enjoy evil, we must return compensation for it. *Rose-Colored Dance* and *Ankoku-Butoh* must spout blood in the name of the experience of evil." (*Rose-Colored Dance* also called *Rosy Dance* is a work Hijikata choreographed in 1965 that we analyze in the next chapter.) Tragedy must take priority over productivity for him, and his body in its immediate sense of physical danger, is already prepared. *Sacrifice* guides his belief that dancers are the ones who experience surrender with their own bodies in a visceral form. Paradoxically, Hijikata's was a dance of sacrifice exposed to public view – while completely rejecting dance for display and entertainment. By this, one can understand how Hijikata believed his dance must stand as a ritual offering at the crucial point where "nature bleeds." In some sense this explains his sacrifice not only of the human material of dance, his half-starved, exposed and emaciated body, but his sacrificial use of animals also – particularly chickens. This sacrifice comes in the guise of love and apology:

> For days I slept holding a chicken and taking care not to eat it. Boyhood hunger is vivid: the chicken my father held was red.... This chicken which laid an egg in the green room played a vital part in my initiation into love. I sometimes visited this partner of mine at a poultry shop in Asahaya. The first time I danced my self-portrait, at a dance studio in Nakano, I started sobbing out loud. I shrieked and eventually foamed at the mouth. That was the first accompaniment to my dance. I apologized to the chicken I held while dancing. Hunger must have been the theme of the universe

(2000a: 39)

Dance is not a matter of understanding, Hijikata writes, his dance has to be made into experiences, taking responsibility for the terror of truth through sacrifice: "The dance, which is a medium between a spirit and impulse to a secret ritual for the sake of pouring into the flesh and blood of young people, ends in finishing them as lethal weapons that dream" (2000b: 47). Here he jumps from "lethal weapons" in his use of terrorist talk to the soft language of dreams, a surrealist jump to be sure, frustrating the boundaries of the mind. Art as experience is more than art as symbol or inference; direct experience is the aim of art that goes by the name of "Experience" in the avant-guard of Hijikata's day. Shock, terror, and wonder are his experiential avenues, and as he tells us, his aim is to open the limits of living material: "I attempt to press the limits of myself and my material. From the nature of my work, living beings are my material" (Ibid.).

It is also clear from his writing that Hijikata is motivated by altruism and love, specifically the attempt to give voice to those on the margins of society. He believes that the *Dance Experience* comes into existence through love giving songs to those who don't have voices. This spirit that he adopted politically from Genet transfers intact to his *Ankoku-Butoh* – as in 'To Prison', *Hijikata* quotes from Genet's *The Thief's Journal*: "Talent is courtesy with respect to matter; it consists of giving song to what was dumb. My talent will be the love I feel for that which constitutes the world of prisons and penal colonies" (1969:110–11).

In his writing, Hijikata shifts from prisoner and terrorist, to lover, spiritual mendicant, and more. He explains his view of dance by discussing dancers' attitudes or spiritual preparation, elucidating a method and technique as he works it out experimentally. His statement in 'To Prison' gives an explicit description of his political ideas and feelings about dance at the beginning of the turbulent 1960s:

> I am chewing on cries and the profundity of esoteric gestures by gazing closely and unceasingly at the mundane. I am inventing a walk modeled of the present from atop the dark earth where dancing and jumping could not be united. In boyhood the dark earth of Japan was my teacher in various ways of fainting. I must bring to the theater that sense of treading. I am a naked voluntary soldier who forces this treading to confront the handling of legs that have been domesticated by floors.
>
> (2000b: 48)

Hijikata states a theme on death and killing in 'Inner Material' that also surfaces in his dances: Goda Nario sheds light on Hijikata's view as he explains a kind of butoh ethics – that clubs are a more compassionate way to kill than bombs and guns (Fraleigh 1999: 174). The implication is that one should have to look the enemy in the eye, and cannot distance from killing. Or as Hijikata put it originally: "Tragedy must be given precedence over production or it is just too frivolous. I remember how intensely lonely I felt when they all laughed at me for saying that we absolutely had to chop heads with a hoe" (2000a: 38).

In 'To Prison', Hijikata writes that he lives "adolescence" in Tokyo "like a dog of an inferior breed while always sniffing out criminal-like fellows." We see how he plays with words to bring the physicality of movement and body memories to language. He thinks only of bleeding, he says: "My eyes never look at anything else." He associates his own body with "bleeding nature" and the pain of living, as this phase of his thinking overflows historical and social categories. Hijikata finally reaches the conclusion in 'To Prison' that his acquaintances in Tokyo are part of a transparent and mechanical world having nothing to do with the bleeding of nature. He sees them as corpses. "Dance," Hijikata says, must have the seriousness of bleeding, and Western dance is incompatible with his desire for "a dance of flesh and blood" (2000b: 43). This period represents an early stage of his search for a personal ethnology in his art. His physical limitations, curved arms and legs of uneven length, would be challenges for any dancer, but he uses his body and physical handicaps ingeniously, by turning his dance in the direction of imperfection. Not stopping at this, however, Hijikata steps beyond his obvious limitations, transforming unexpectedly, streaming consciousness from image to image.

THE CRIMINAL AND THE FOOL: WRITING/LIVING DARKNESS

Tohoku is the starting point for Hijikata's world of darkness – a home for his words and dances in an originative sense. More than a place or landscape, it is the metaphysical unseen structure that compels his embrace of darkness. In '*Kaze Daruma*', we gain an understanding of the darkness that compelled him, not an evil force as it is so often characterized in the West, but rather a trust in the truth of primal experience.

> In the early spring the wind is something special, blowing over the sloppy, wet mud. Sometimes in early spring I would fall down in the mud and my child's body, pitiful to its core, would gently float there. I try to speak but it's like something has already been spoken. I have the feeling there is a knot of wood, somewhere in my lower abdomen stuck there in the mud, that is screaming something. While in the mud, it occurs to me that I could very well end up becoming prey. At the same time that this unbearable feeling surfaces in my body, something strange takes shape in the mud. It's as if my body had, from its very core returned to its starting point.
>
> (2000d: 73)

'*Kaze Daruma*' (Wind Daruma) is a lecture originally titled "*Suijakutai no saishu*" (Collection of Emaciated Body) and given in February, the night before the Tokyo Butoh Festival 85. This was subsequently published as '*Kaze Daruma: butoh zangeroku shusei*' (Wind Daruma: Collected Record of Butoh Confessions) in *Gendaishi techo* in May 1985. Hijikata died almost a year later on January 21, 1986 at Tokyo Women's Medical College Hospital from hepatocirrhosis and liver cancer at the age of fifty-seven. Shortly before his death he danced in the film *Mikiko Monogatari* (Mikiko's Story, 1986), as the custodian of a small shrine for *Kannon*, the Buddhist Goddess of Mercy. He amuses and talks to her throughout the film; then in the end, disappears into the river holding the statue of *Kannon*, having morphed by the time of this work from his pose as a surrealist criminal to the figure of the divine fool.

In his writings and performances, he was a work in process, guided by his desire to retrogress to "a frog's view" as he called it, mining genuine words intuitively from his body. At the end, Hijikata rose to infancy; sat up and danced on his deathbed for those closest to him – his dance the beauty of ugliness – his words messages from the dark spot of consciousness. Ohno Yoshito, who visited him in the hospital at the time of his death, says Hijikata told him the only thing he feared was God. Yoshito was struck by the ambivalence of this because Hijikata had "grilled" his father Kazuo often and quarreled with him about the existence of God. Present at the beginning of Hijikata's career and still there at the end, Yoshito reports Hijikata-the-disbeliever's final words: "In my last moments, God's light. . ." (Ohno and Ohno 2004: 137).

BODY AS SPIRIT: WRITING/SPEAKING THE BUTOH BODY

Although Hijikata never professed a spiritual tradition, his last workshop encouraged students to disperse into *Nothingness*, a key concept in Buddhism. Kasai Akira, Hijikata's collaborator during the early days of butoh, also teaches butoh with an unacknowledged Zen flavor, juxtaposing contradictory images for students to experience in dance (Fraleigh 1999: 248). The butoh that Hijikata stirred in himself and his inheritors shares a Zen Buddhist, surrealist, and Jungian belief in the healing potential of the subconscious mind. Negativism in Butoh, like the nothingness (or emptiness) of Buddhism, can clear away personal history to allow being (itself) to shine. But we know that butoh is not Buddhist by design; it operates more theatrically as a kind of "dance Dada," edgy and playfully absurd. Martin Esslin traces relationships through the serious play of the Dada (or Dadaist) art movement in Europe (early in the twentieth century) – through German Expressionism – to early Brecht and surrealism. And along with Eugene Ionesco, he also notices how the puzzling irrationality in the procedures of the theater of the absurd closely resembles the Japanese Zen koan paradox in its defiance of rational terminus (Esslin 1961: 315).

We do not suggest that butoh resurrects the existentialist theater of the absurd or relates consciously to Zen, but it does contain historical residue. However original, butoh has a memory, kinaesthetic and imagistic, as well as methodological. Butoh relates to surrealism in its improvisatory spirit, its expressiveness, polemics, and eroticism. Andre

Breton states the immediate or automatic, improvisatory method of surrealism in his famous surrealist manifesto of 1924: Surrealism is "a pure psychic automatism" by which thoughts are expressed directly in writing or any other form. His manifesto provides a methodological definition of surrealism, as there are also other ways of looking at this complex art movement that we examine throughout this volume. Esslin writes that while in Germany the impulse behind dadaism and expressionism had flagged by the middle twenties, and the whole modern movement was swallowed up in the intellectual quick sands of the Nazi period in the 1930s, the line of development continued unbroken in France (Ibid. 274). A recent article on surrealism (past and present) defines it in the context of social space as "political culture" (Strom 2004) echoing the rebellious, skeptical stance in which Hijikata danced.

Japan has had a long history of body culture and writing about the body, contrary to the views of Western observers like Mark Holborn who says that, butoh "...took place in a culture that, unlike Western classical tradition, had no history of the body at the center of either aesthetic or philosophic preoccupation" (Holborn 1987: 12). We know this isn't true! The body *has* been conceptualized in Buddhist intellectual and spiritual history that far outstrips Western views. Contemporary Japanese philosophers Ichikawa Hiroshi and Yuasa Yasuo draw from that history, and they modulate it with current phenomenological concepts of "the lived body," East and West.

Ichikawa and Yuasa deal with the concept of the "lived body" from an Eastern perspective, one we believe explains how the body is presented in butoh dance styles. Yuasa's celebrated philosophy, *The Body: Toward an Eastern Mind–Body Theory* (1987), draws from Western sources while also inquiring into Eastern *praxis* of self-cultivation. He provides a body-scheme that is Japanese and at the same time comprehensively related to the work of contemporary Western phenomenology. Ichikawa counters Western dualism in his philosophy, employing the phenomenology of Husserl, Sartre, and Merleau-Ponty, and carrying their work further on Eastern grounds. His thesis is that the body we live in is much closer to what we understand by the word "spirit" than it is to matter or biology, as Hijikata's butoh also challenges the materiality of the body through a non-dualistic route. Ichikawa's prominent works *Seishin toshite no Shintai* (The Body as Spirit, 1975) and *Mi no Kozo: Shintairon wo Koete* (Structure of the Body: Overcoming the Theory of the Body, 1993) have not yet been translated into English, but his theories have been introduced to English speakers in Nagatomo Shigenori's *Attunement Through the Body* (1992) and the work of Chikako Ozawa-De Silva (2002). Yuasa and Ichikawa's comprehensive concepts of the body as "unfinished potential" and "body as spirit" provide a philosophical framework for understanding the metamorphic nature of Hijikata's writing/ speaking/dancing. Hijikata's dances, as also his writing and speaking, ensue from a process aesthetic – or what is identified in butoh as "the body that becomes." This is what we are calling "the metamorphic context of butoh," one of its main distinguishing features. Likewise, Hijikata's *butoh-fu*, the word images that guide his choreography (as we explained in the first chapter), also move and molt constantly. Never quite finished, always in the making, words spring from Hijikata in the manner of his dances. At some point, his words distill to text however – as we see in his writings and spoken monologues – just as his *butoh-fu* are finally embodied in dance. Because of this, it is important to distinguish Hijikata's process aesthetic from dance improvisation styles in the West: contact improvisation, improvisation leading to choreography, or free experiment. While it may seem that Hijikata's spontaneity bears a kinship to modern/postmodern dance improvisation, his words are politically motivated and preserved, and his dances are choreographed through *butoh-fu* – as we will take up shortly.

Butoh dancers deconstruct the physical in morphing from image to image and project the body toward *nothingness;* theirs is not an ethereal escape from the body as in the classical ballet of the West. It is a transformative process that accepts change, just as nature (human and non-human) is also a study in time and space, decay, death, and regeneration. Hijikata's butoh starts with a felt sense of body, not from reason or technique, as he writes to his student Nakajima Natsu in 1984, two years before his death in a letter called "To My Comrade" (Hijikata 1984):

> We shake hands with the dead, who send us encouragement from beyond our body; this is the unlimited power of BUTO. In our body history, something is hiding in our subconscious, collected in our unconscious body, which will appear in each detail of our expression. Here we can rediscover time with an elasticity, sent by the dead. We can find Buto, in the same way we can touch our hidden reality, something can be born, and can appear, living and dying in the moment.

If body *is spirit* and spirit is not denatured, as Ichikawa holds, this in turn allows us to understand the body beyond the skin that Ichikawa and Yuasa cite as the "immaterial body" beyond rationalization. This is the body without boundaries that is postulated in Eastern metaphysics and is indeed very suspect in materialist cultures. This is also the butoh body in its metamorphic essence, incomplete, ongoing and perishing in each step, not an essence that we safely resolve nor an object that we conquer as we might strive to conquer nature, but the body as encompassing spirit and enigma.

Ichikawa's "body as spirit" is based on various levels of unity. He claims that our existence itself unifies the spiritual and physical levels. Spirit and mind are nothing but names given to the same reality. The body becomes truly human when the distinction between spirit, mind, and body disappear. Thus a high degree of unity expresses our freedom, while mental disorders are characterized by a low degree of unity:

> When the degree of unity is low and we are controlled by the environment, we have less freedom, we feel the body. The ultimate situation is that of a corpse.
>
> (Ichikawa quoted in Ozawa-De Silva 2002: 27)

Butoh does not express high degrees of unity, as we have seen. Rather the butoh body is porous and suspect.

BEING A CORPSE

Hijikata initiated movement from the feeling of being a corpse, as he often said in his teaching, "Butoh is a dead body standing desperately upright." He puts it this way in *Kaze Daruma:*

> I would like to make the dead gestures inside my body die one more time and make the dead themselves dead again. I would like to have a person who has already died die over and over inside my body. I may not know death, but it knows me. I often say that I have a sister living inside my body. When I am absorbed in creating a butoh work, she plucks the darkness from my body and eats more than is needed. When she stands up inside my body, I unthinkingly sit down. For me to fall is for her to fall. ... She is my teacher; a dead person is my butoh teacher. You've got to cherish the dead. Because we too, sooner or later, some day far or near, will be summoned, we must make extraordinary preparations while alive not to be panicked when that time comes.
>
> (2000d: 77)

In terms of Ichikawa's philosophy of the body, the butoh dancer presents a low level of unity that brings the dancer closer to the body through the realization of death and the struggle of uprightness. While the ballet dancer practices upright control over gravity, butoh practices the metaphysics of *becoming* in a metamorphic process. The butoh body is only partially constructed as Hijikata indicates in his dances and makes explicit in 'Fragments of Glass' (2000e), first published as 'Language as Lack and Temporary Construction of the Body' in 1977. Ballet moves upward in its airy grace and ethereal disappearances. Butoh tends toward disappearance also, but it moves downward, plying awkwardness and dissipation, and as with material nature, it can regenerate.

HIJIKATA'S *BUTOH-FU*: WHAT IS AN IMAGE?

An image is often understood in terms of visual material, pictures, photographs, and figures in paintings, something discernable to the eye, but images are actually much more than this, as the study of butoh reveals – especially the *buto-fu* of Hijikata. His imagery is drawn from a wide variety of sensory sources, including the appeal of words. "Images," as the word suggests, come from and also reflect the imagination. Finally in performance, the dance we see and relate to is itself composed of images, movement images, sometimes called dance images, phrases and larger gestalts of movement resulting from choreography or improvisation – as explored extensively in *Dance and the Lived Body* (Fraleigh, Part 3, "The Dance Image," 1987). There are many layers of images in butoh, those that inspire the dance, those that animate its metamorphosis, and the actual images that strike the eye and mind of the audience.

Nowhere in dance do we find such a rich exposition of imagery than in the work of Hijikata. Hijikata did not perform on stage after 1974. He concentrated on choreographing for others and also worked extensively with Ashikawa Yoko. Gradually he recorded his original dance notation, or system of *butoh-fu* – sixteen scrapbooks of verbal and visual images for dance based on his experiments with surrealist strategies from poetry, painting, and literature. Kurt Wurmli who has studied the scrapbooks extensively says the eclectic assemblage of visual images in Hijikata's collection range from prehistoric cave paintings to twentieth century street graffiti, including works from all five continents. "The images are partially or entirely cut out and glued-in reproductions of works of art, nature, architecture, and science in the form of photocopies, prints or

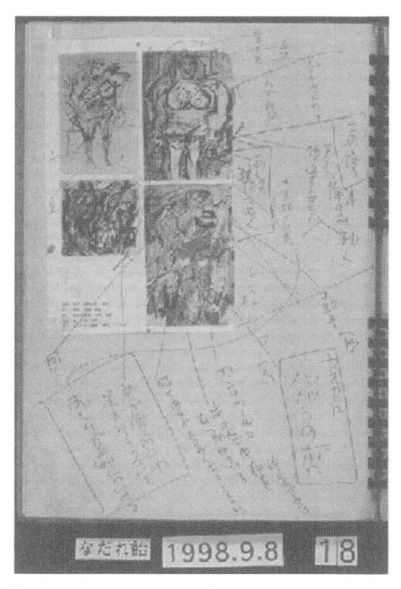

Figure 2.2 Hijikata's *Butoh-fu* "Dribbling Candy". Courtesy Hijikata Tatsumi Archive

hand drawings. In all, they make up a collection of over 500 individual works" (Wurmli 2004: 7–8).

Hijikata's imagistic style of recording dance provides a basis for present-day understanding of the origins of butoh in surrealist imagery. Wurmli reports that Hijikata did not date his work; thus, the exact time period and order of the books are uncertain. Hijikata started the *butoh-fu* in the early 1970s and finished them in 1985. They contain Hijikata's writing, his marks, and the collected visual images. The text itself is handwritten in poetry and phrases, and most of it relates to the visual materials. The marks, mostly in pencil, are lines, circles, arrows and the like, used to emphasize parts of a visual image (Ibid.). We can see from this that Hijikata's *butoh-fu* is a collection of highly complex verbal and visual images intended as an illustrated poetic guide for dance movements. For the most part, the images themselves (also called *butoh-fu*) do not show exact postures or movements, but leave this open to discovery – except in a few cases where actual photographs of dance are shown.

Butoh-fu can be defined most basically, then, as visual/poetic images used as the basis for butoh movement and gestures; they are sometimes referred to as notation used to guide the dancer or inspire dance movement and choreography. Butoh performers and teachers, from Hijikata and Ohno to those who came after them, use *butoh-fu* to instruct dancers. Those close to Hijikata, such as Ohno Yoshito, Tamano Koichi, Kobayashi Saga, Nakajima Natsu, Ashikawa Yoko, and Waguri Yukio, use images related to Hijikata's *butoh-fu* to shape their dances, and often as a basis of their butoh classes, as we will explain further in Chapter 4. Wurmli reports that the applications of Hijikata's butoh-fu are demonstrated in videotapes taken from lectures and workshops held at Keio University and displayed in the "Permanent Installation". From the English-language introduction "Hijikata Tatsumi's Butoh: Experiment and Upheaval of Dancing" to the festival catalogue *Tatsumi Hijikata's Butoh: Surrealism of the Flesh, Ontology of the 'Body'* (Wurmli 2004).

Ash Pillar Walk (Hai-bashira no hokou) and *Bug Ambulation (Mushi no hokou)* are two examples of *butoh-fu* created and taught by Hijikata. These are evocative words that bring images to mind in terms of vision, movement, and processes of imagination. Put more succinctly, they are "visualizations" that can be experienced improvisationally or structured choreographically. *Butoh-fu* have existential implications also: These authors have experienced *butoh-fu* as explorations in "becoming an image," embodying the image, and not simply mirroring it mimetically as impetus for movement. In a 1992 class that Sondra Fraleigh took with Waguri, students became lightning, chickens, and bee pollen. Waguri uses these typical *butoh-fu* from nature and other sources, not simply to inspire movement, but to teach dancers how to embody imagery. Butoh dancers do not bring lightness and floating into their bodies in imitation of pollen, because butoh movement is not imitative. Over time, dancers can let go of the self (the will) to *become* the floating and get lost in puffy lightness. Similarly, butoh dancers who draw upon Hijikata's *Ash Pillar* experience their bodies as diaphanous columns of flesh – as ash moving impossibly on the edge of disintegration – as pillars that can't stand up no matter how hard they try. Mikami Kayo refers to the "Ash Pillar Walk," as a movement that Hijikata compared to the walk of death-row inmates on their way to execution, or the walk of children forced to sit still for many hours whose legs have fallen asleep (Mikami 1993: 84–91). She explains the ash pillar as a human sacrifice that has been burned, so that the only thing left is ash ready to crumble at any moment. When the ash figure walks, it has lost any power to control itself and moves erratically. *Bug Ambulation* sets in process an existential experience of eating and being eaten – one bug morphs to millions moving in the tree outside the body (the dance) – and inside the body (the dance) – itching the flesh – eating the flesh – eating consciousness – until only consciousness remains.

It would not be correct to say that *butoh-fu* are meant to stand on their own. As original collages of visual/poetic images, they provide the notational basis for the movement and stillness of butoh. *Butoh-fu* can be described from various standpoints: the dancer's embodiment of the image, the surrealist construction of the image, the collage relationship of poetic text to pencil marks and visual art, as visualizations exploring imagination, and as notation for performance and historical preservation of choreography. Once set in motion, *butoh-fu* exceed their visual/verbal designs and take on another life in dance. The movement that emerges can also be called an image, since dance movement is shaped in time and space. Dance can be conceived and understood through the unfolding design of visual/kinaesthetic movement patterns (images) that reveal the lines and forms of the dance. These are the movement images of the dance, and they carry lived valences (values) whether emotionally neutral or highly charged.

The literal meaning of *fu* in Japanese is chronicle (a written history passed from generation to generation), notes, (music or dance notation), also score; thus, a *butoh-fu* is not necessarily a set of choreographic instructions. Hijikata took the word in his own direction, but did not invent the term. In the original spirit of a chronicle, *butoh-fu* will differ from dancer to dancer in format, style and meaning. In Hijikata's *butoh-fu*, there are numerous variations of arbitrary forms as identified by Baird's (2005) analysis. Based on the overlap of commentary of Hijikata's dancers on the structure of his later dances and the release of Hijikata's notebooks, an arbitrary methodology emerges including elements such as instructions, forms or movements, character-types, and narratives. The following example of a *butoh-fu* from a workshop by Kobayashi Saga in which Tamah Nakamura participated on November 26, 2003 illustrates the form and movement element of Hijikata's method. Kobayashi, who joined Hijikata in 1969, presented as an original member of *Asbestos-kan* and part of the *Hijikata Tatsumi Exhibition* at the Okamoto Taro Museum that included workshops by Hijikata's disciples.

In Kobayashi's workshop, Nakamura did not experience all of the elements that Baird identifies, since in any dance practice, they may not all be included; Hijikata's *butoh-fu* are not meant to be presented in a linear order. Kobayashi's workshop takes place on a section of a dance floor with the same wood and dimensions like that in Hijikata's studio, *Asbestos-kan*. Following Baird's analysis of form and instruction, the heading (indicated below) is the name of the form. Under the heading, each instruction is followed by suggestions on how to achieve the form, either physically or imaginatively.

An Old Woman

Bent back, crouching	Knees bent, back lowered, and feet grounded low into the floor, gnarled arms bent hanging down in front of you.
Eyes unseeing	Eyes are covered with cataracts; vision blurs and pupil appears white.
Desire to walk forward	The image and feeling of attempting to reach for a pencil just out of reach on the floor in front of you.

To create the quality of an old woman in the dancers' movement, these instructions present increasing levels of abstraction from physical to imagistic.

Disciples' notebooks of *butoh-fu* recorded during practices with Hijikata were on display at the exhibition. These contain many entries similar to those of the sixteen scrapbooks on file at the Keio University Research Center for the Arts and Arts Administration. Hijikata did not date his collection of *butoh-fu*, so archivists may have numbered the scrapbooks based on the date of magazines from which Hijikata cut photos or paintings. They contain copies of photos that Hijikata used to help dancers create images, accompanied by handwritten phrases and line drawings to emphasize the visual material. In fact, Hijikata did not publicize his own *butoh-fu* until just before his death in 1985. Waguri Yukio, the main male dancer at *Asbestos-kan* from 1972, has used his *butoh-fu* notebook of Hijikata's practices to create *Butoh-Kaden* CD-Rom – the only published version of Hijikata's method available as of this publication. Waguri's *Butoh-Kaden* CD-Rom and booklet (1998) does not give instructions, but illustrates the imagery of butoh, and short snapshots of dance forms or movements.

With all the attention on Hijikata's *butoh-fu* and attempts to capture his structure and method, Kobayashi says that no completed choreography was ever recorded because Hijikata would change it in the final practice just before the performance, and there was not enough time to write it down. Thus, there are no *butoh-fu* in existence for any of the final performances that Hijikata choreographed. This is also true of Ohno Kazuo's performances, since they are also based on images – and Ohno's own kind of *butoh-fu*, however carefully structured, are always alive to the improvisational moment.

WORDS THAT DANCE: OHNO'S IMAGES

The essential thing in dance is that it haunts and clings to your body the same way that your lifelong experience has.

(Ohno Kazuo)

As we noted earlier, a *butoh-fu* is not a set of instructions or method on how to do butoh. The literal meaning of *fu* is a chronicle or history, therefore any dancers' spoken or written chronicles of their process, in whatever form, is their *butoh-fu*. According to the Ohno Kazuo Archive in Yokohama, there are a very large number of Ohno's *butoh-fu* in existence currently being categorized at the archive. The archive is not yet open to the public.

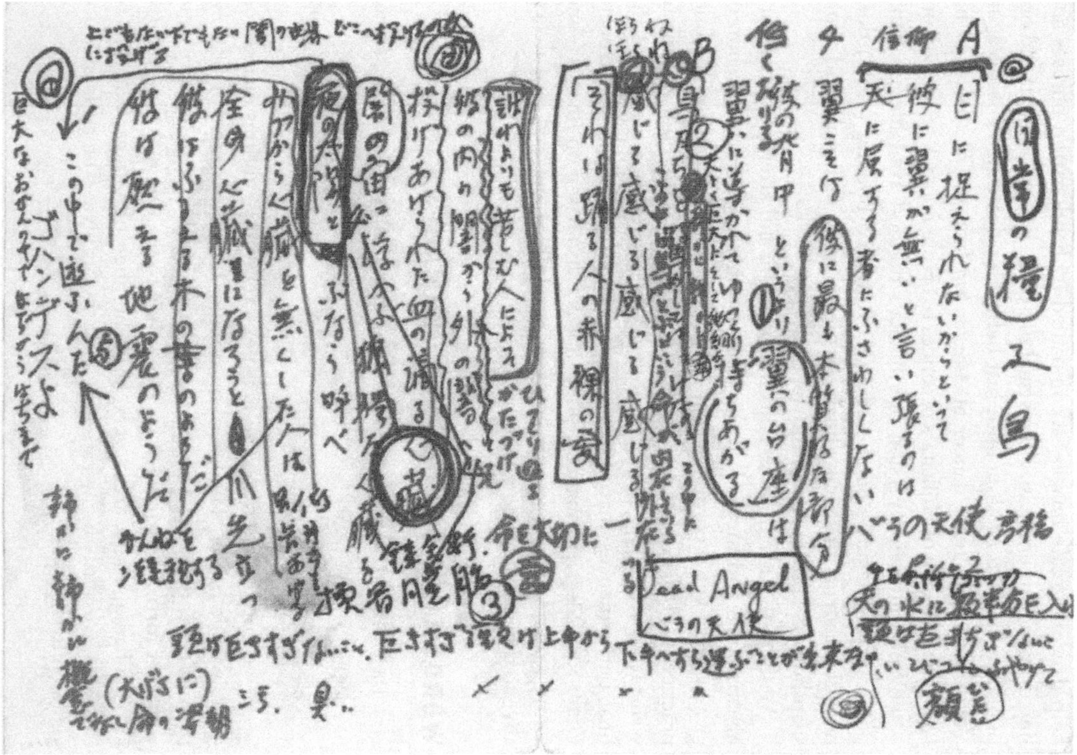

Figure 2.3
Ohno's *Butoh-fu*,
a photograph of
his calligraphy
and marks.
Courtesy Ohno
Kazuo Archive

Ohno's words in *butoh-fu* and workshop talks are in essays, poems, and notes that he prepares for performances and workshops.

Hand
> When does it come?
> Where does it come from?
> Whose hand?
> The invisible hand that responds to words
> (Essence of eroticism).
> > (Ohno's *butoh-fu* for "Episode for the Creation of Genesis"
> > – Part of his performance in *The Dead Sea* (1985))

The *butoh-fu* above represents the type of short poems Ohno writes on the blackboard or pieces of paper in his dance studio when he is practicing for a dance. He jots words down in the form of ideas and rough sketches on specific themes during the course of his daily life as they come to him.

Butoh practices influenced by Ohno are presented in Chapter 4, while here we focus on his poetic writings and workshop talks, which are verbal reflections in preparation for performing and teaching. He explains:

> Basically, "butoh" means to meander, or to move, as it were, in twists and turns between the realms of the living and the dead. The human hand has evolved in such a way that it is well able to talk. Its "speech" can finely articulate all that we feel.

> (Ohno and Ohno 2004: 205)

SPIRITUAL DARKNESS: INSIDE OHNO'S STUDIO AND *KONPAKU*

Nakajima Natsu, one of the female founders of butoh, gave a pivotal speech at Fu Jen University in Taipei in 1997 explaining a Japanese Buddhist perspective of spiritual darkness in the work of Hijikata and Ohno and its feminine basis, even though these dancers were not working literally within any religious tradition. She takes us inside Ohno Kazuo's studio and his workshop word *Konpaku*. She says that many foreigners come to Ohno Kazuo's studio, and he gives them a phrase to dance on. For example, "Dance in the heavens. Dance in hell. Dance in the heart." Most people can do this and feel good about it, Nakajima says. But when Ohno says dance in *konpaku*, all of a sudden they don't know how to move. *Konpaku* is a word that even the Japanese have forgotten and would be startled by. It describes the riverbanks where the dead and the living come and go, very much at peace. Nakajima emphasizes that the Japanese use Buddhist terms like *higan* – the far side of the riverbank for the world of the dead, and *shigan* – the near side of the riverbank for the world of the living. *Konpaku* is where the dead come and go several times a year crossing the river to their ancestral homes. It is not a place, but "nowhere out there." She says we can call this darkness, spirituality, something formless, the unconscious, or the destroyed and disappeared. This is something that cannot be seen – something that Ohno identified as *Konpaku* and Hijikata called *ankoku* and *yami* (shadowy darkness) – emanating contradiction and irrationality (Nakajima 1997).

HOW OHNO PREPARES: WORDS FOR THE SPEECH OF THE BODY

Kazuo's words are vehicles for the speech of his body, just as his dances are universal moments in self-realization that are common to all who identify with the overflowing life he represents. Kazuo's words and dances draw from his Japanese Buddhist ethnicity, his life as a Christian, his spirituality, and two women – his mother and La Argentina. His *butoh-fu* are existential questions, spurred first by war, and later by a self-imposed reclusive period after which he came back to the stage to perform *Admiring La Argentina* in 1977. Kazuo articulates a philosophy of life through evocative poetry and movement drawings, *butoh-fu* open to interpretation and embodied in his dance. Yoshito explains that expressions such as "God is great" or "Thank you," are not verbalized by Kazuo, but are nevertheless expressed in his butoh (Ohno Yoshito 1999: 23). Yoshito feels that Kazuo's dance lives in his words and body speech, especially his hands, as they dance a harmonious combination of the Orient's soft arts (like brush painting) with the West's voiced eloquence (Ibid. 89, 97).

Ohno's philosophy of dance is directly related to life. He opens one of his butoh workshop talks this way:

> Please begin each workshop by telling yourself that dance isn't something remote from your day-to-day lives. ... The essential thing in dance is that it

haunts and clings to your body the same way that your lifelong experience has. Does that gesture tell us something about a wound you once suffered?

He continues with one of his frequent themes, our obligation to honor the dead:

The sufferings of others have, without our ever fully realizing it, been engraved in us. Let me put it this way. We survived only because others died in our place. ... Don't rest on your laurels; it's utter nonsense to believe that you are life's be-all and end-all.

(Ohno and Ohno 2004: 298–9)

In another workshop, Ohno encourages personal dance styles and somatic feelings of freedom:

We've got to explore the reality of our feelings. Well, then, we've almost come to the close of today's workshop. For the remaining five minutes *free style*, yes, *free style*, all the while bearing in mind that our personal feelings color our reality.

(Ohno and Ohno 2004: 258)

In Tamah Nakamura's interview with Yoshito in March 2005, he explains how his father creates words, "My father writes in words, and while in the process of writing, he creates his own universe. He does not create while moving or practicing in the dance studio. He creates his movement and creates his own universe while writing. I think that would be his uniqueness. He doesn't change or modify at practice." An example of one of Ohno's poems as a creation of his universe is his reflection on his *Dead Sea* performance recorded in his publication of *The Ishikari River's Hooked-Nose Salmon* (2002: 60):

The universe gave birth to the universe
Life from the sea created a new life
The sun, the light, the darkness
I was there
They collided and burned
At that very moment
   I was there.

Yoshito says that his father's words give him ideas and provide time to reflect before a performance. (We can't help but notice that this would

be similar to the silent meditation a Noh actor does just before performing.) Kazuo's *butoh-fu* emerge from pure spirit. He also uses them in
practice to teach students in workshops. Kazuo says, "Look at this
drawing, and move like this and then improvise." In his book about his
father's butoh and life, Yoshito describes Kazuo's approach to creating
words: Kazuo looks at portrait paintings, and reads poems and *haiku*. He
writes in colored pens, repeatedly erasing and re-writing on large sheets
of paper. He has dreams during this time. Kazuo thinks, "Am I dreaming
or am I going into a dream?" Through this process, expressions come
naturally on his face; this is the process in which words come into the
unconsciousness. Then he practices moving while reading what he has
written (Ohno Yoshito 1999: 13). Until the moment of his performance
on the stage, he always looks at his *butoh-fu*. But as soon as he is on the
stage, he disregards it. If he sticks to *butoh-fu*, he cannot perform spiritually; yet, until the moment right before the performance, he looks at it.

Ohno's jottings and memos are much more than simple notes on
paper or the blackboard suggesting technique or approach to the dance.
Ohno is also a poet. He expresses his inner life in poetic phrases, as he
prepares for his dances. In preparation for his performance of *Suiren*
(Water Lilies) he reflects on Monet, who painted *Water Lilies* at a time in
his life when his eyesight was already weakened. How might Monet have
seen his canvas and his flowering subject? Ohno puts himself in Monet's
place:

> I could no longer see the visible,
> I could see the invisible,
> The hands of the soul reached me.
> The eye of the soul opened,
> Wrapped my whole body,
> Leaving me, touching me.
> My hands and mouth moved and danced.
> (Ohno Kazuo 1992b: 69 in *The Palace Soars Through the Sky*)

As we will see in Chapter 3 in the analysis of *Suiren* (Water Lilies), Ohno
is aware of eyes all over his body, and when doing his makeup, he
accentuates his eyes with thick black eye liner. His dance is not simply an
imitation or interpretation of Monet's *Water Lilies* canvases. Ohno's
poetry on Monet distills a transparent understanding of how the "words"
of his hands and mouth *move* in dance.

If Ohno's poetry helps create his universe and reality, the poetic waxes into movement as the images help create the body, the flesh (*Karada o sozo suru*). Yoshito explains possible meanings of body in Japanese as *nikutai* (flesh), *shintai* (physical body), *karada* (body), but only the word *karada* includes *kara*, which also means emptiness in Japanese. Yoshito says:

> Yes, *Kara*. Well, the word *sora* (sky or body) can also be written with the Chinese ideograph as *karada* (body). *Karada*. There is nothing: *Karada*.

Ohno's book *Butoh-fu: Goten Sora o Tobu* (The Palace Soars Through the Sky 1992b) is one of three of his publications presenting his words. It is a collection of his essays and work notes including stage directions. Another important book of *butoh-fu* is *Dessin* (Ohno Kazuo 1992a), a published reproduction of his hand-written *butoh-fu* for *Ishikari no Hanamagari* (The Ishikari River's Hooked-Nose Salmon, 2002), an open-air performance that took place on the banks of the *Ishikari* River in Hokkaido in September 1991.

THE ISHIKARI RIVER'S HOOKED-NOSE SALMON

Ohno Kazuo's poetry is translated by Nakamura Yoshihiro for this Routledge publication. (To differentiate Ohno Kazuo and Ohno Yoshito, we use their first names in this section.)

Dessin, as we just mentioned above, is a portfolio publication of Kazuo's choreographic notes on the performance of *Ishikari no hanamagari* (The Ishikari River's Hooked-Nose Salmon). This portfolio presents an excellent example of what Kazuo's poetry means to him and how it relates to his dances. Performed on September 15, 1991 by Kazuo and Yoshito at the mouth of the *Ishikari River* in Ishikari, Hokkaido, the performance is composed of segments of Kazuo's dances such as: *Vienna Waltz, Red Table, La Argentina*, as well as a *Prayer to Ishikari River*. The portfolio contains words, poetic phrases, and line drawings in preparation for the performance. There are no photos, surrealist paintings, or magazine clippings. His *butoh-fu* are his own thoughts on the setting, costumes, and movement, accompanied by sketches of hand movements and dance notations for moving across the stage.

As Kazuo stands looking out over the mouth of the river, the setting for his four o'clock to sunset performance, he writes:

The mouth of the river,
Jammed with floating logs,
I am not lonely.
I'm in a happy moment
With family.
(2002: 39 in *Hooked-Nose Salmon*)

In *Dessin* (1992a: Unpaginated), Kazuo sketches salmon flapping from scaffolds upheld by poles – slashing on the page in strong, bold calligraphy brush strokes. A copy of this sketch in *The Ishikari River's Hooked-Nose Salmon* accompanies Ohno's *haiku* poetry of nineteen syllables in three lines of 3/7/9 (as translated in English):

Salmon swim
Against the river current,
Looking for the origin of life.
(2002: 34, 35)

As his thoughts turn to costumes and the body as costume, on the left-hand side of the page Ohno sketches, but his hand-brushed poetry speaks of thoughts beyond material:

The costume the soul has on
Is flesh
Is universe,
Flesh speaks for the universe.
(1992a: Unpaginated in *Dessin*)

Peel off skin
Kill flesh
On the road
Lay them down.
(Ibid.)

Kazuo reflects on the flow of life and death – and the womb as world:

Which is a boat?
Which is a river?
Interwoven life and death.

A baby holds on to mother,
A mother to her baby
In the flow of the river.
　　(2002: Forward in *Hooked-Nose Salmon*)

Mother's womb
Everyone experiences.
Only babies can feel
Shyness and naiveté
Growing in an unknown world.
　　　　(Ibid. 36)

Kazuo does not write his *butoh-fu* to create a method but to prepare psychologically for a performance, musing on the setting, costumes, body movements, and stage movements. Dancers and scholars have not yet begun analyzing his *butoh-fu*, as they are doing with Hijikata's. Kazuo's phrasing, while not in the classical form of Zen *haiku* poetry with its seventeen (or less) syllables of 5/7/5, is as simple, classic, and brief – expressing pure spirit. The essence of Kazuo's mindfulness is reflected in his words after his performance of *Hooked-Nose Salmon* in an interview with Kobayashi Azuma, *Dessin* publisher (1992a: 4):

Thought is reality
Reality is thought

Kazuo's *Butoh-fu* in *Dessin* focus on public performances, and present the working methods used in his famous dances. We find a different perspective on Kazuo's 'words' in *Keiko no kotoba* (Workshop Words), which contains extracts from his workshop words audio taped by many of his students. This publication includes five chapters of Kazuo's spoken words at workshops – his creative workshop talks. These talks might be considered fragments of loose thoughts in spoken form; in the creative process, they provide reflective periods for new birth to be experienced.

In Kazuo's childhood home, and in his present home with his wife and Yoshito, they have a Buddhist altar. All the same, some of the family along with Kazuo have been baptized Christian and attend church. As with many Japanese, multiple religious affinities co-exist. Kazuo's mother not only prayed at her Buddhist altar but attended church whenever she could. Yoshito said that he asked Kazuo to show him only once how

Figure 2.4 Ohno Kazuo and Yoshito dance a typical duet in *The Dead Sea* (1985). Yoshito's more somber presence grounds Kazuo's flowering movement and delicate gestures. Both figures will transform as the dance progresses and Ohno takes on a more masculine presence toward the end.
Photograph by Ikegami Naoya.
Courtesy Ohno Kazuo Archive

being Christian is connected with being a butoh artist. Kazuo replied that he would travel to Bethlehem on a pilgrimage back to his spiritual birthplace, "as if Christ is walking" (Interview with Nakamura, March 2005). The actual pilgrimage culminated in the performance of the *Dead Sea* (1985) danced by Kazuo and Yoshito. Hijikata choreographed Yoshito's dance in this performance, but it was about Kazuo that Hijikata commented after the performance: "Finally a spiritual butoh dancer came to us."

Yoshito sees traces of his paternal grandfather, Ohno Tozo, in *The Dead Sea*, especially Kazuo's masculine performance in formal black attire in a section of the dance (Ohno and Ohno 2004: 126–7). Kazuo's father Tozo was a fisherman with the salmon fleet on the Sea of Okhotsk; thus, we see that Kazuo's connection with salmon as a theme is rooted in his childhood. His father spent long months at sea with the fishing fleet, and on returning to Hakodate liked to pass time at a local geisha house. As the eldest son, Kazuo would often have to go and fetch his father in the morning from the geisha house, where he would find him chanting along with the *Gidayu* (chanting with shamisen) players. Because of his father's long absences, Kazuo grew close to his mother (Ohno and Ohno: 126–7).

We see that Kazuo's words and dance themes are drawn from his life, but they don't stop there. He holds that dance is spiritually transformative, and does not necessarily recreate daily life. If it starts with daily work and can account for messiness, it is nevertheless special; through dance you can experience ". . . a blossoming in yourself. You will become a flower. You will become a lotus" (Kazuo in Ohno Yoshito 1999: 133). Kazuo's poem for the *Dead Sea* performance illustrates his flower motif as transformation:

> The hand is the rose of the flower
> The arm is the stem of the rose
> (Ibid. 193)

In Kazuo's *butoh-fu*: "The Palace Soars Through the Sky" (1992b: 24–5), he shares his poetic reflections on life in his lecture and performance at Cornell University in 1985:

> Am I writing about daily life?
> Am I writing about butoh?

My mother's womb?
The womb of the universe?
I am not sure.
My space of butoh is my mother's womb
And the womb of the universe.

Kazuo's words are more than mere questions; through his poetry, he reflects on what his dance experiences have meant to him, not only as a person in his own life, but also as a member of humanity, perhaps as our human representative in the universe – as Kazuo says:

The body is already the universe.

(Ohno Kazuo with Dopfer and Tangerding (in conversation) 1994)

BODY AS UNIVERSE: KAZUO AND YOSHITO SPEAK OF LOVE AND CARE

For the development of butoh, Ohno Kazuo's spiritual *butoh-fu* create a space for dancers to explore their movement universe 'free style', as he likes to instruct. Kazuo's words and dances also influence the development of butoh by creating poignant tension between social obligations and human feelings in a transcendental mode that does not make sharp distinctions between the stage and daily life. La Argentina was not simply a Spanish dance performer for Kazuo to emulate. Coaxing butoh out of darkness and into the light, in his workshop words he says:

I was anxious because I didn't know how I was going to join La Argentina. How could we possibly unite again, given that I had to keep treading over pile upon pile of dead bodies? When, in the end, I couldn't take another single step, La Argentina reached out her hand to me. Words such as "sorry" or "thanks" come nowhere near expressing my gratitude for her kindness. Because the love she embodied wasn't merely that of a solitary human being but that of the whole world, of an endlessly expanding universe of love and care.

(Ohno and Ohno 2004: 267)

Kazuo's words reach out with innocent spontaneity and generosity. When Sondra Fraleigh saw him dance *Suiren* in Yokohama in 1990, she was moved by how he gathered the audience to him at the end of the dance, embracing them whole, his large expressive hands folding into his heart as he bowed. In his words and dances Kazuo embodies a transcendent love, and by that we don't mean something otherworldly. Since this chapter is concerned with his words, we observe how Kazuo's words serve his works and are based in life, on the women in his life in the instance of *Argentina* and *My Mother*, on paternal qualities in *The Dead Sea*, and on nature – rivers, fish, birds, and flowers. Kazuo's themes also come from the hardships of his life, especially his survival of eight and a half years as a soldier before and during World War II, beginning in China, spending the last year (some accounts say two years) as a prisoner of war in Menakawari, New Guinea. (During these long years, Ohno rose to the rank of Captain in charge of provisions.) Then came his long difficult return to a destroyed homeland.

Yoshito was three months old when his father was conscripted for military service in August of 1938 and nine when he returned. These were the brutal times that tested Kazuo's gentle spirit and honed his respect for life. Extending himself to a universal other in his dances, Kazuo touches something in audiences that allows them to realize an ideal form of love, what in Kazuo's Christian ethos would be called *Agape*. This form of love is about giving, while *Eros* is motivated by desire, the fulfillment of each through the other, and *Filia* is brotherly love. Kazuo's dances give unconditionally. Audiences respond in various ways, some feel grateful for their lives, many cry, feeling healed in his presence and through his dance. The meaning of Kazuo's dances and words – their poetry and character – get lost in his being. In performance, his spontaneous giving spirit abounds.

Yet people who know Kazuo sometimes comment on his aloofness, and indeed this may actually serve his art, even as some objective distance is required of any performer. As to his personal character offstage, as usual his son Yoshito, who has contributed tremendously to the words of butoh, has the last word. Underneath Kazuo's sometimes-cool veneer, there is love and gentleness, as Yoshito says: "Kazuo's warmth and tenderness are not those of flesh and blood. The form of love he epitomizes pierces the public's heart" (Ohno and Ohno 2004: 125–6).

3

DANCES OF DEATH, SACRIFICE, AND SPIRIT

Sacrifice is the source of all work and every dancer is an illegitimate child set free to experience that very quality.

(Hijikata Tatsumi, *Inner Material/Material* (2000a: 39))

TWO BUTOHISTS: WHY THEY DANCE THE WAY THEY DO

Japan, like many regions of Asia and the "melting pots" of the West, has developed diverse aesthetic and political/religious configurations, and in many cases has welcomed change. Hijikata himself, while decrying the Western colonization of Japan, used the creativity he garnered from German *Neue Tanz* and European surrealism to invent his "Body in Crisis." Theater dance in today's Japan is diverse, ranging from the traditions of Kabuki and Noh to Japanese development of Western ballet and modern dance – and still the continuing evolution of butoh. Dance critic Tachiki Akiko says that butoh often slides into the work of other new dance in Japan (Daiwa International Butoh Festival, London, 2005). So how do we know butoh when we see it in the twenty-first century, and does it still bear a relationship to butoh founders, Hijikata Tatsumi and Ohno Kazuo? Nakamura Fumiaki (1993) calls the current, new performers of butoh "butoh dancers" because they emphasize the beauty of butoh as choreographed performance. However, those who maintain the spirit of Hijikata and Ohno's butoh, Nakamura terms "butoh-ists."

Clearly, Hijikata and Ohno provide the term "butohist" its original meaning and restive force. From the very beginning, Hijikata and Ohno intrigue audiences as much as they baffle them. In several ways their butoh is like all dance in this regard. Dances don't tell stories, except in the tales of ballet and in narrative forms, and even then the stories are seldom literal or linear. Narrative in dance, as in the early modern dances of Martha Graham, is cast in metaphors and symbols that peak the body's deep responsiveness to kinetic images. To dance is to explore human consciousness through bodily means.

Hijikata and Ohno invert consciousness, however, sublimating the body while extending its liminal states, as we explore in analyzing five of their dances in this chapter. These men are not narrative or symbolist modern dancers; neither are they neutrally postmodern. As butohists, they move past modern categories altogether. One does not so much read their butoh works to find meaning there; rather, one enters into morphing states of awareness through the performances. There is a difference between metaphoric and metamorphic imagery; butoh does not ride on metaphor, but rather on change and an *ethos* of becoming. As the root word of ethics, *ethos*, points to a matrix of values, attitudes, habits, and beliefs. Here we refer to a cultural disposition that appreciates the ongoing nature of life and the life/death/life cycle, never-ending in solid form, because it comes from emptiness, itself not really empty, but in process of emptying and filling, like the process of breathing.

Meaning in butoh comes through one's *experience* of the dance, and not from deciphering a message or choreographic intent. Surely there is an element of subjective reflection in being an audience for any kind of dance, but Hijikata and Ohno are the first to proffer wholly experiential avenues for relating to dance. *Hijikata's offering comes in the form of sacrifice; Ohno's comes through reverence for life and the healing of trauma.* Hijikata dances his darkness, constructs his body of pain and absurdity, and the audience morphs through these aspects of themselves. As for Ohno, people feel better in his presence and through the spirituality of his performances. The audience for butoh is offered an experience of theater that is not distanced – filtered through centuries of movement styles and character development – as in Kabuki and Noh, or even Western ballet. As Japan's first butohists, Hijikata and Ohno circumvent the abstractions of modern dance and transcend the neutral pose of Western postmodernism.

Now students of dance have access to an experience of Hijikata's butoh through his *butoh-fu* (his notation, as we took up in the previous chapter, and will revisit in our final chapter) and can learn how to work with metamorphic imagery in a similar vein. Seeking a direct route to butoh experience, dancers and actors from around the world still come to Ohno's workshops in Yokohama, even as his son Yoshito now teaches them with Ohno approaching his 100th year and in a wheelchair. Some say they make the pilgrimage to Yokohama simply to be in Ohno's presence – as these authors learned through speaking with several of Ohno's students and in taking his workshops. (For Fraleigh's accounts of taking Ohno's workshops, see 1999: 57–64, 164–5.)

DANCE AS EXPERIENCE: SHEDDING THE SOCIAL BODY

Experience, as such, guides Hijikata and Ohno. They dance human experience in broad strokes as they connect to life and death. In their shapeshifting, they become other creatures and explore elements of nature, even as they poke holes in the political world stage they inhabit. It will become apparent, as we look into their dance works that they are searching for something underneath the human skin of society – Hijikata through his challenge of social conventions and connections to his childhood, and Ohno through his spiritual brand of depth psychology.

We do not examine their works for symbolic content and meaning, but rather for their personal, social, and political context, and their dark/light reversible structures. Hijikata's *Ankoku Butoh*, as initiated during the rebellious atmosphere of the 1960s, is admittedly political, and it can also be described as a globally oriented social movement. Emerging first in Japan through Hijikata's *Dance Experience Recitals*, as a criticism of Western culture and political dominance at a time of violent social protests against the Japan–US Security Treaty (AMPO: *Nichibei Anzen Hosho Joyaku*) and the Vietnam War, this early butoh is referred to as *gishiki* (ritual) in Japanese media reports of the time. The early butoh of Hijikata and Ohno can be interpreted on one level as an anti-social resistance movement effected through a deconstruction of the social body. Hijikata and Ohno were certainly aware of the social issues of their time and how the body is culturally conditioned or constructed.

Their dance attempts to question, deconstruct, shed, or deform the body's cultural conditioning – to excavate experiences of the native human body, also called in butoh "the body that has not been robbed." There are other interrelated perspectives on the body that are important in butoh. These come from the idea of representing the trauma of the war and its resulting social memory through the body (Igarashi 2000: 168–9) and from considering the performance of desire through "physical nostalgia" in an experimental form (Sas 1999: 176). Such readings of the butoh body through trauma and desire extend beyond those of violent rebellion, anti-social behavior, and bodily deconstruction. Butoh is not the product of a single event, nor can it be reasoned through a single social lens; it can be explained less reductively as a form of dance experience and a social movement emerging through two talented men in the opportune environment of creative freedom. Even as we focus on Hijikata and Ohno, it becomes increasingly clear that Ohno's son Yoshito, Waguri Yukio and three important women – Motofuji Akiko, Ashikawa Yoko and Nakajima Natsu – also contributed to the founding and perpetuation of butoh.

The presentation of the butoh body as a form of social rebellion converged with an aesthetic tendency toward Obsessional Art in 1960s Japan. Revivals of surrealism, neo-dadaism, expressionism, existentialism, post-war social upheaval, and demonstrations against American political and economic hegemony all played a part (Kuniyoshi 1990). Japanese art after World War II derived from action and developed around issues of the body and place. Physical and site-specific works examined the relationship of the appropriate body expression with the elements of place and environment (Osaki 1998; Munroe 1994). Like Jackson Pollock's modern art in America in which he threw paint on the canvas to get his body viscerally involved, the anti-social movement and art in Japan were action-oriented, placing importance on the temporal process of experience. Underground street theater or *Shogekijo* (Little Theater) developed at the same time in response to the perceived need for expression of social issues by and for the people. These itinerant groups performed in tents and small theaters in an attempt to recapture the popular entertainment of pre-canonized Noh and Kabuki Theater. Influential groups included *Aka Tento* – Red Tent, and *Jokyo Gekijo* – Situation Theater; *Tenjo Sajiki* – The Gallery; *Kuro Tento* – Black Tent and *Waseda Sho-gekijo* – *Waseda* Little Theater.

Thus, avant-garde art and theater opened a social gap for Hijikata to create a new form of "ethnic dance" through his *Ankoku Butoh*. Dance historian and butoh critic Kuniyoshi Kazuko sees that Hijikata's butoh stems from a concept of the body called *suijakutai*, literally "weakened body," or the body that you sense living in your body other than your present self (Kuniyoshi 2002: 64). Hijikata says that his dead sister lives inside his body, scratching away the darkness inside him when he dances (2000d: 77). For him *suijakutai* confirms the existence of the origin of self farthest from modernism (Kuniyoshi 2004a). New is not necessarily better; the movement of old people, introverted and slow tempos can all be beautiful. Western dance celebrates youth; while in contrast, Hijikata and Ohno reveal a full spectrum of human experience, not just the Japanese experience. Their dance figures are empathetic and openly affective, not perfect.

CHALLENGING MODERNIZATION

Hijikata wanted to create what he called Tohoku Kabuki, in restoring the original, local intent of Kabuki before the Westernization of Japan. The social context for the emergence of butoh through Hijikata and Ohno had its antecedent in the history of Kabuki, particularly the movement to reform Kabuki as the influence of the West expanded in the *Meiji* period beginning in 1868. With the aim of rejuvenating the Kabuki tradition, 'civilization and enlightenment' (*Bunmei Kaika*) became guiding principles for the theater reform movement in the early *Meiji* period (Tschudin 1999: 83). The establishment of the Ministry of Religious Affairs effectively placed all actors and entertainers in government service as teachers to educate the masses and to 'encourage virtue and chastise vice' (Tschudin 1999: 84). Kabuki gradually became monopolized and institutionalized by large corporations. European artistic techniques and radical political ideas produced actors who were no longer suited for the Kabuki stage. *Shingeki* (New Theater) was then created as a stage for expression of multinational theater ideas and by 1960 was dominant in Japanese modern theater (Lee 2002: 377).

The *Seinen Geijutsu Gekijo* (Youth Art Theater) was formed in 1959 when *Shingeki*, which was really Western-inspired theater serving a dominant text, itself became establishment theater, and could not respond to the perspectives of young people. One of the early underground dramatists, Kara Juro, leader of *Jokyo Gekijo* (Situation Theater), developed his group as a pre-modern Kabuki troupe of itinerant actors producing a bawdy vaudeville act (Goodman 1971: 163). Transcendence of the modern age was one of the concepts of contemporary Japanese theater out of which Hijikata's butoh was born. To challenge and revolutionize modernization, a new language was needed that recognized and shifted the fallacies of established policies and laws. Thus butoh was fundamentally political. As an example of one of the new aesthetic languages, butoh also exhibited characteristics of the original Kabuki's folk appeal as well as Kabuki's representation of the dark side of social life (Klein 1988: 16–8).

Butoh has been described quite differently from classical and modern forms in Japan and abroad. Western and Japanese discourses in the English and Japanese media over the past forty-five years have held butoh in an image of resistance through deconstruction, death, and grotesque body forms. In Japanese performance reviews over four decades (1961–2003), butoh is described using terms such as *ankoku* (darkness), *zen-ei* (avant-garde), *waizatsu* (chaotic, vulgar), *angura* (underground), *kimi no warusa* (creepy), *kitanasa* (dirty), *boryoku-sei* (violent), *erotisizumu* (erotic), *konton* (chaotic), *anaakii* (anarchistic), *kikei* (deformed), *igyo* (uncanny), *tosaku-teki* (transvestite), *keiren* (trembling), *shinpiteki* (mysterious). Butoh reviews first began appearing in the *New York Times* around 1984 after groups such as *Sankai Juku* and *Dai Rakuda Kan* performed abroad. Butoh is commonly described in the *New York Times* and other US-based newspapers as grotesque, hallucinatory, painful, decaying, startling, destructive, insane, and dislocating. These authors believe such partial valuations interpret only the surface look of butoh. A close look at dances of Hijikata and Ohno will take us more deeply into the subjects and experiential approach of butoh, as we describe and analyze five works in chronological order, including an extensive note on a recent film of Hijikata's *Summer Storm*. Our own experience of these dances informs the text where possible, and we include experiences of others that are available to us through published accounts.

KINJIKI (FORBIDDEN COLORS, 1959)

Hijikata dared to go against the safely coded lyric and dramatic modern dance that developed in Japan through the influence of the West. In so doing, he ushered in Japan's postmodern dance in stark dramatic tones. In his first dance, *Kinjiki*, performed for the Japanese Dance Association

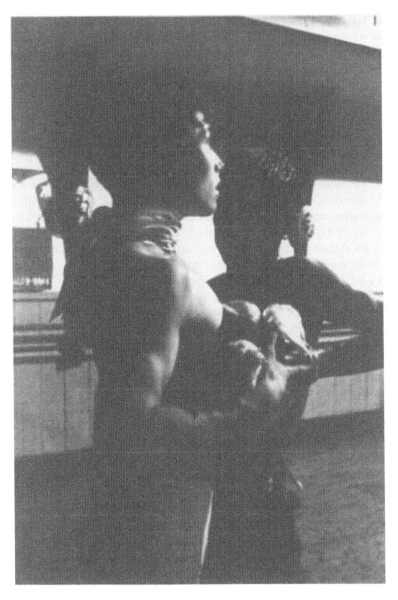

Figure 3.1 Hijikata and Yoshito in rehearsal for *Kinjiki* (Forbidden Colors, 1959). Photograph by Otsuji Kiyoshi. Courtesy Hijikata Tatsumi Archive

in Tokyo (and described briefly in the first chapter), Hijikata surrenders to what analytical psychologist Carl Jung calls the shadow side of life. In *Kinjiki*, as in later work, Hijikata is interested in looking death and forbidden feelings in the face, acknowledging the experiences these stir in him, and transferring the experience directly to his audiences. *Kinjiki* was controversial in this respect. Some audience members attested their release of dark emotions and a therapeutic connection to the dance, as Goda Nario remembered (Goda 1983), while others were disgusted. Through this dance, Hijikata eventually left the Japanese Dance Association.

Forbidden Colors is the English title for *Kinjiki*. We have only been able to mention that Hijikata's inspiration for this dance was the Japanese literary master Mishima Yukio and his book *Kinjiki* with homosexuality as one of its themes. After 1970, the year of Mishima's suicide, Hijikata's work shifted to a new register, completing its liberation from Western dance movement altogether and finding a unique notational vocabulary based on pictorial and verbal imagery that he called *butoh-fu*. By then, Hijikata was learning how to dance the various selves and hidden images of his subconscious, excavating his sister there and admitting his childhood terrors. He also began to choreograph extensively for others, consciously including women and feminine energy in his work.

In its raw beginnings, at the dawn of the politically driven 1960s, Hijikata's *Kinjiki* was exclusively masculine with its forbidden theme of homosexuality and referred to bestiality as well, though audience accounts were not in agreement about this aspect. The chicken squeezed between Ohno Yoshito's thighs was later sacrificed in the dance. The cruelty, however shocking, might have seemed mild to Hijikata at that time, in light of the chaotic, defeated world of post-apocalyptic Japan. What the audience is left to sort out *in their experience* of *Kinjiki* is the same question that American playwright Edward Albee explores in *The Goat, or Who is Sylvia?* – his Tony winning play of 2002, where the main character falls in love with (guess what) a goat! In love with a goat? This is the rub! And why allude to bestiality on stage? Albee was born in 1928, the same year as Hijikata, and although American, he writes in the same surrealist, political vein as the European authors who inspired Hijikata, Samuel Beckett and Jean Genet with whom Albee is often compared.

Now we ask, is Hijikata just a country bumpkin who blindly fraternizes with farm animals? Or is he an artist who is often in agony about his relationship to the land and his ethnicity? The latter implies one's relationship to country, land, people, race, and the human body, even as animals are represented there. Certainly he is aware of the strong societal taboo against bestiality. In his characteristic, intentionally crazy surrealist stance, he tests the audience in this regard. These authors also believe that Hijikata's pre-occupation with chickens and animal imagery *per se* is emblematic of his search for identity in the midst of the spiritual crisis of Japan after the war. Death and life were large issues then, perennial ones in any case, and Hijikata was a man in search of his identity. When he performed *Kinjiki*, he was thirty-one years old, poor, and still adjusting to Tokyo in post-war Japan. In staging a totem animal sacrifice, he proceeded much as shamans have often done, moving toward the dark regions of subconscious life, projecting this into visible performance. It is clear at this time, that he is not seeking admiration for his dancing, rather he seems to be taking upon himself the mantle of the dancer-shaman, harking back to his childhood roots and testing social boundaries. His intent to shock his audience awake is apparent.

Kinjiki is a dance of darkness in several ways. The stage itself is darkened: Yoshito, Ohno's young son, dances in dim light with Hijikata, and they mime sexual attraction at points – looking deeply into each others' eyes. Kurihara Nanako, who interviewed Nario Goda about the work, describes it briefly from his account of seeing the dance and his article about it (Goda 1987: 41–2). He describes the dance as a ritual sacrifice. Hijikata portrays *Man* with bell-bottom trousers and a shaved head, using black grease on his face and upper body. As the *Boy*, Yoshito wears a black scarf around his neck and lemon-colored shorts. They dance barefoot. After the boy appears on stage, the man, holding a chicken, enters and runs in a circle. The boy stiffens, and walks to a narrow illuminated area center stage, where the man is waiting in the darkness. Breathing hard, they face each other, and the man thrusts the chicken into the light with the white wings fluttering "stunningly." The boy accepts the chicken, turns his head, and holds it to his chest. Then placing the chicken between his thighs, he slowly sinks into a squat, squeezing it to death while the man watches from the darkness. (Not everyone believes the chicken dies.) The boy stands in shock, and the audience is outraged. When they see the chicken lying at the boy's feet, they gasp. Black out (Kurihara 1996: 54–5).

In the second half, as Goda remembers, the dancers perform in total darkness with the audience hearing sounds of breathing and moaning.

The boy runs, and the man chases him. Toward the end Yasuda Shugo plays bluesy jazz on a harmonica, and the stage brightens slightly. "The boy walks away, dragging his feet and holding the chicken in his arms" (Ibid. 55–6). This partial description aims to capture the costumes, movement on stage, and the physical sounds of the dance. *Kinjiki* has been interpreted in different ways: as dark, masochistic, abusive, homoerotic, ritualistic, sacrificial, strong, quiet, stiff, withheld, and as both beautiful and ugly. Perhaps all of these apply in view of personal perception and differences in audience perspectives. Hijikata is never simply linear or obvious. He textures *Kinjiki* with *pathos* and the complexities of masculinity, as also in subsequent work, he becomes increasingly more able to exhume from his own body a theater of hope and misery, stemming from his childhood with a tyrannical alcoholic father who beat his mother.

Hijikata ran, he says, chasing after his mother as she tried to escape these violent episodes. He felt helpless, and eventually dissociated by visualizing his home as a "theater" (Ibid. 23). One senses this sublimated anguish in Hijikata's portrayal of "Leprosy" (a section of *Summer Storm*, 1973) with its trembling emotional shading and quiet forbearance. *Kinjiki*, as Hijikata's first butoh, also paints a tremulous inner landscape – though perhaps not as skillfully articulated as "Leprosy" – where Hijikata's subtle body shifts seem to transform the very space around him. This incredible power of Hijikata as a performer cannot be captured in a photograph or verbal description, and it seems to have been there from the beginning – with *Kinjiki*.

Many who see Hijikata perform report how he viscerally enthralls them. Motofuji, who later becomes Hijikata's wife, and is in the audience for *Kinjiki*, says she feels "electricity run through her body." Dance writer Miura Masashi reports in his article, '*Hijikata Tatsumi no kyofu*' (Fear of Hijikata Tatsumi), that Hijikata's performances make him "tremble" and his hands sweat (Ibid.: 43, 58). At the same time, Hijikata's works offer the audience a space to texture emotional engagement – even as his exploitation of fear is mollified by bitter sweet and tender contrasts. There are beautiful episodes of slow restrained movement in *Kinjiki*. Eternally slow continuously morphing movement – not unknown in Japanese traditional forms such as Noh Theater and the spare aesthetics of Zen meditation – eventually mark a butoh signature, surfacing, paradoxically, in Hijikata's first choreography.

The chicken, however, is most remembered in accounts of *Kinjiki*. The dancers' attitude toward the chicken displays both the experience of love and violence. Hunger is perhaps the over-riding theme. The wary chicken, playing its part as an object of hunger, crosses over categories of food, sexual hunger, and spiritual longing. This is a famous chicken: *Kinjiki* with its three performers, Hijikata, Yoshito, and the chicken, separates Hijikata from the then known dance world in Japan – and also the 1960s postmodern dance in the West, which turns increasingly toward neutral, unemotional pedestrian forms. There is nothing else like *Kinjiki*, and for the rest of his life Hijikata continues to develop the archetype of the rebel in butoh.

BARAIRO DANSU (ROSE COLORED DANCE, 1965)

In November 1965, Hijikata and Ohno performed *Barairo dansu: A LA MAISON DE M. CIVECAWA* (Rose Colored Dance: To Mr. Shibusawa's House) at *Sennichidani Kokaido*. This is a group dance choreographed by Hijikata with a duet section for himself and Ohno – also featuring Ohno Yoshito, Ishii Mitsutaka, Tamano Koichi, and Kasai Akira. Nakanishi Natsuyuki, a well-known painter, and Yokoo Tadanori, an accomplished graphic artist, also collaborated in this performance. The stage scenery of this dance is vivid and morphs considerably – from a fortune telling chart in front of which a dancer fences in full attire, to a scene with a vagina painted on the back of dancer Tamano. This realistically painted image opening the outer lips and folds to expose the inner design of female sexuality covers Tamano's entire back. Hijikata is more often identified with the erect phallus he later wore in *Rebellion of the Body* (1968), a costume also copied by other butoh dancers, but here he reverses his sex and gender glance. In *Rose Colored Dance*, the stage is decorated with drawings of human internal organs and female genitals drawn in graphic detail.

There is also a pedestrian scene with a barber cutting hair on stage, as three men sit in a row of chairs wrapped in large striped towels, much as one might find in a Tanztheater work of Pina Bausch. Ohno Yoshito and Kasai Akira are in the dance. They perform wearing briefs, their nude bodies spattered with muddy chalk, as they dance with plastic tubes, blowing and looking through them, wrapping up in them, and creating striking shapes with their preoccupation.

Hijikata and Ohno dance a satirical duet in white dresses, their dance caught in photographs now widely published. Hijikata sometimes emulates Ohno's movements and they indulge suggestions of intimacy. We

Figure 3.2
Group photograph of *Barairo Dansu* (Rose Colored Dance, 1965). Photograph by Nakatani Tadao. Courtesy Hijikata Tatsumi Archive

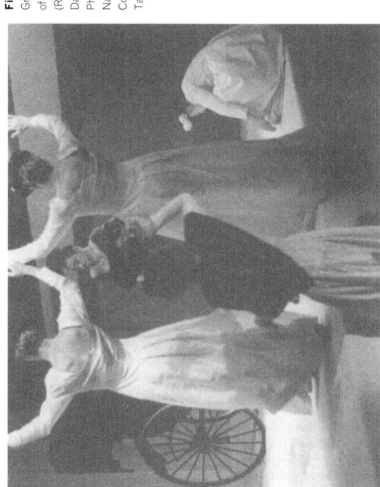

know that in their daily life, however, their relationship was not intimate but rather formal, and Hijikata deferred to Ohno's maturity as elders are respected in Japan. As artists they were exploratory; in *Rose Colored Dance* they performed in playful embrace, smelled each other's feet, and roiled in mischief, rolling on top of each other. They were in effect *experiencing* each other, not in the physically neutral manner of contact improvisation as it developed in the West, but directly, through touch, smell, and intentional association. Their dance while not overtly sexual was rebellious in flaunting taboos of sexuality and the body, but it was still somewhat under the influence of movements from the lyric modern dance they both had studied.

Incomplete videos and films of the dance show its irony and edgy playfulness. Hijikata and Ohno wear matching white Western style gowns, simply cut with scoop necklines and sewn with gathers around a drop waistline. They dance unassumingly in the dresses, not to parody women, but simply to be themselves, moving together and apart, foregrounding each other's movement, and tangling at points. Ohno Yoshito states that this dance fulfilled a wish of Hijikata's to dance with Ohno in a similar costume and to share his movement (Ohno and Ohno 2004: 134). Hijikata writes of Ohno's contribution to his dance: "Mr. O. [Ono Kazuo], a dancer of deadly poison and a pioneer in experiential dance, an awe-inspiring teacher and a friend, helped carry my dance works to the theater. He is both a cabinetmaker and a poet who, with a fond gaze, singles out every work of unhappy heartburn" (2000a: 39).

Hijikata explains the sacrificial impulse behind *Rose Colored Dance* when he revisits his failed efforts at Western dance techniques, and vows to prepare an antidote – "a dance of terrorism," his way of demolishing dance for display. In technique classes he endures "the jockstraps and Chopin" of Western dance, and throughout it all "the diarrhea of misery." In spite of his negative feelings, Hijikata reports that he continues to go to the theater in his early days in Tokyo, and that it gradually dawns on him from this position that "audiences pay money to enjoy evil." He conceives *Rose Colored Dance* to compensate for that. We can see this in his comparison of the "rosy" and "dark" sides of his work:

> Both the "rose colored dance" and the "dance of darkness" must spout blood in the name of the experience of evil. A body that has kept the tradition of

mysterious crisis is prepared for that. Sacrifice is the source of all work and every dancer is an illegitimate child set free to experience that very quality. Because they bear that obligation, all dancers must first of all be pilloried. Dance for display must be totally abolished. Being looked at, patted, licked, knocked down. A striptease is nothing to laugh at.

(2000a: 39–40)

NIKUTAI NO HANRAN (REBELLION OF THE BODY, 1968)

In 1968, Hijikata choreographs the work that marks *Ankoku Butoh* as a new genre. His dance *Hijikata Tatsumi to Nihonjin: Nikutai no hanran* (Hijikata Tatsumi and the Japanese: Rebellion of the Body), also known as *Rebellion of the Body* and sometimes *Revolt of the Flesh*, is performed at *Nihon Seinen Kan Hall*. This shamanist dance, signaling Hijikata's maturity as a surrealist and his further embrace of the subconscious, is symptomatic of the inner turmoil through which he is living; his preoccupation with personal identity as a native son of Japan from the remote Tohoku region finally explodes. His concern for explicating culture has been building. In June of 1968, he performs in *Ojune sho* (Excerpts from Genet), a recital given by his student Ishii Mitsutaka. Hijikata dances *Hanayome (neko)* (Bride [Cat]) in a kimono. He also dances *Kirisuto* (Christ), and later develops these dances into episodes of *Rebellion of the Body* in October that same year.

Antonin Artaud's *The Theater and its Double* was translated into Japanese in 1965 and had a profound influence on a new generation of Japanese directors and performers including Hijikata. This is evident in the directly experiential aspects of his work and the anarchy of *Rebellion of the Body*. In this work, Hijikata under the influence of Artaud and still in the thrall of Jean Genet, enters the stage through the audience, borne on a palanquin, a long kimono covering his naked body, and in his hand he holds a golden phallus – as in Artaud's *From Heliogabalus, or The Anarchic Crowned*. Hijikata transforms episodically through several scenes in this concert length work, morphing from the demonic to the satiric, waving a large strapped-on golden penis, dancing as a man in a gown, and binding himself with ropes in crucifixion, his sleek and browned body wrapped in swaths of white cloth. The wildness of his long hair and beard seem to mock the short pink dress and ankle socks he wears in a

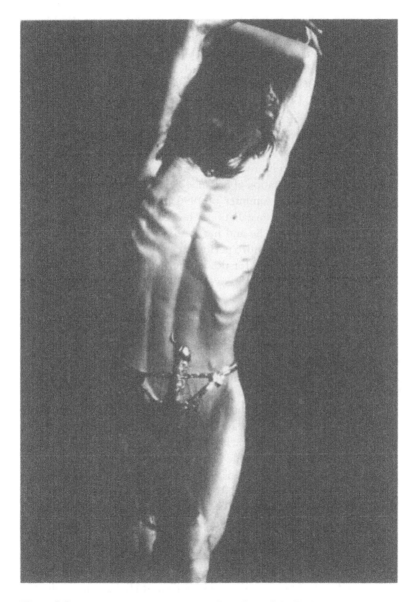

Figure 3.3 Hijikata in *Nikutai no hanran* (Rebellion of the Body, 1968)
Photograph by Torii Ryozen. Courtesy Hijikata Tatsumi Archive

particularly absurd scene. In another, he dances violently in a long heavy gown, his movements reminiscent of the waltz and tango. Western and Japanese elements coexist in clashing collage and spasmodic movement. It is through this work, performed nearly a decade after his first radical experiment *Kinjiki* (1959) that Hijikata's butoh is gradually understood as a new form of dance born of his memories of the poverty and mysticism of Tohoku.

But he in no way returns to a simple past; rather he fastens on the present indelibly by scattering Western costumes and dance styles along the path of descent to his own Japanese roots. Sondra Fraleigh saw an installation film presentation of *Rebellion of the Body* at the Asian Museum in San Francisco in the summer of 1996. Hijikata's costumes for the dance were part of the installation. She remembers watching people come and go, and that she and her husband were the only audience members to stay for the entire performance. People seemed baffled by what they saw, unprepared for the surrealist tactics of Hijikata and the raw energy of his dance. Many covered their eyes or mouths, or looked at the floor.

One of the most startling images of the dance that appears so often as an image in books of butoh photography is that of Hijikata, an erect metallic penis strapped to his groin as his only costume, reaching his arms around his head to enclose a sideward glance. Characteristically, he sucks in his abdomen – all the more to expose the bony structure of his emaciated rib cage. We know that he prepared himself for this dance through fasting and tanning his body under artificial light, leaving his skinny body shining like a dagger with mystery and daring. When Hijikata criticizes the "lethargic fat" society of Tokyo, he says, "in such a case the penis will never become a radiant dagger" (2000a: 40–1).

What is he trying to say to us through this phallic dance, audiences have wondered and critics pondered? Does he himself seek some revelation? Some healing transformative secret to unravel? Or is he simply provoking us, as artists will, to experience our bodies more sharply? If we consider precedents in the West, especially the Greeks through Dionysus and the horny satyr, we see, without any trouble, several related explanations for Hijikata's strapped-on penis and those phallic dances of Tanaka Min and others who followed Hijikata in butoh. The exaggerated phallus, represented in Greek plays by comic actors and satyrs, is also admired and feared in the God Dionysus, who was always a pesky outsider in the Apollonian, Platonic world of perfect form. In other words, Dionysus is the *Other*, not necessarily the male other in terms of gender, but the sensuous other, as a deeply feminine and flawed God imported from the East. Historian Thomas Cahill in *Why the Greeks Matter* tells us that "Dionysus, almost certainly a homegrown Greek god going back to earliest times – but also the epitome of Otherness – was always spoken of as a foreigner, an intromission from the effete East" (Cahill 2003: 202).

As a challenge to social mores of the Japanese, Hijikata (as satyr) acts satirically – even as the Greek god Dionysus would – to enliven the sight and soul of forgotten otherness in his audience; and through the subconscious region of darkness that is also Dionysian, he probes rejected shadows of erotic vitality. Now this is not necessarily to embrace evil, even though Hijikata says he wants to "go to prison" in a rebellious turn of mind, to be caught "smack in the middle of a mistake" (2000b: 45). More it is to ward off evil, by staring it in the eye, as was also the function of the satyr. There is a not-so-fine-line between the vital desires that compel people in love, fear, and conquest, and the crossover into evil doing. Hijikata apparently understood this, and he wanted to blur the line, so as to make the darkness more evident. He was certainly willing to risk being *Other*, the social outcast, in the name of his dance.

His most immediate model for this was the original bawdy Kabuki before it was purged of folk vulgarity for Western audiences, but we know that Hijikata also studied the West. He admired German author Friedrich Nietzsche's writing from the nineteenth century and understood the Dionysian and Apollonian values interlacing Nietzsche's *Birth of Tragedy*, harbinger to twentieth century European existentialism. In 'To Prison', Hijikata quotes Nietzsche's view of work: "My work is to reanimate with vitality a skeleton pieced together from the consciousness of being a victim. I am a man of simple sensual passion. The sense of the tragic increases and declines with sensuousness." In the next breath, Hijikata quotes German born American philosopher and political theorist Herbert Marcuse in *Eros and Civilization*, also on the subject of work: "Work is *a priori* power and provocation in struggle with nature; it is the overcoming of resistance." Hijikata's provocation he says in his own words is "dance." His goal in dance is an existential answer to Nietzsche (whose philosophy had already borrowed a great deal from the East) and Marcuse (a thinker who also transcended Western categories). Cast in assimilation of their language, Hijikata's goal in dance is, as he says:

... to open up the current situation with hands that hold a chalk eraser which wipes out signs of an impotent future, of that culture of mournful cries which exist in the skeleton of victim consciousness. I am placing in the body of my work an altar similar to asceticism in front of a human body purged of impurities.

(2000b: 47)

Hijikata's *Rebellion of the Body* can be understood in terms of East and West, and how he synthesizes them in surrealist dance. He maps his semi-starved erotic body in the process, becoming the forgotten other, but not to forget his childhood terrors and Japanese "earthbody" in the wake of Western technocracy and domestication of the body. He says after the war, and twelve years of living in Tokyo:

I am chewing on cries and the profundity of esoteric gestures by gazing closely and unceasingly at the mundane. I am inventing a walk molded of the present from atop the dark earth where dancing and jumping could not be united. In boyhood the dark earth of Japan was my teacher in various ways of fainting. I must bring to the theater that sense of treading. I am a naked volunteer soldier who forces this treading to confront the handling of legs that have been domesticated by floors.

(2000b: 48)

Hijikata's dance assimilates archetypal human experiences of the dancer shaman, the cheated victim, the rebel, the satyr, the crucified martyr, and the wounded child, bearing his audience finally toward an experience of the impeccable, naked political warrior, fighting with righteous indignation for a life of simple sensual passions. Of the latter, he says: "My work is to remove toy weapons from the limbs of today's youth, who developed in barren circumstances, and to finish them as naked soldiers, as a naked culture." One is reminded of an earlier time and the naked beginnings of modern dance in Hijikata's statement – that Rudolph von Laban at the foundations of *Neue Tanz* in Germany advocates dancing nude in nature for benefits of health and the recovery of human expression. Hijikata's nudity, however, comes in the guise of combat.

NOTE ON *NATSU NO ARASHI* (SUMMER STORM, 1973)

Arai Misao brings Hijikata's *Summer Storm* to light in a 2003 film and DVD of a 1973 performance at Kyoto University in Japan (Arai 2003).

The footage of *Summer Storm* that Arai took in 1973 sat in a can for thirty years, he said, until he looked at the dance again, realizing that there were few complete records of Hijikata's dancing and choreography. He didn't want to interfere with the integrity of the dance by editing it. He did however commission new music by YAS-KAZ to respect Hijikata's style, also showing city scenes of Tokyo to introduce the dance, and at the end summer snow (Arai in conversation with Fraleigh). As the film finishes, pulling away from the dance and snow in sunshine, it fades gently to the sea and land of Japan, shooting Tohoku from the air in stunning views.

The film captures one of Hijikata's last performances in public and his incredible embodiment of "Leprosy" in two sections. It is also important as a record of one of Hijikata's most mature works as a performer and choreographer, showing clearly delineated movement and compositional structures. As a concert length work, *Summer Storm* develops episodically and is choreographed by Hijikata for his company members, all of whom have carried his butoh legacy forward as choreographers and performers: Ashikawa Yoko, Kobayashi Saga, Tamano Koichi, Waguri Yukio, and Hanagami Naoto.

As a dance of prayer, *Summer Storm* is a gift from Hijikata's poverty – a haunting, mesmerizing work of quiet struggle and compassion, its somber tones also offset with playful skittering elements, as in the scene: "Young Girls Picking Herbs." Significantly, *Summer Storm* lays to rest questions about the influence of war in Hijikata's choreography. It is clearly anti-war, addressing death through the names of places where many died in World War II in a section called: "Dreams of the Dead, the Sleep, the War." Hijikata narrates this part, speaking over the dance in his poetic way, such lines as: "Sleep oh Sleep . . . Iwo Jima . . . The sea of Midway." (The battle of Iwo Jima was one of the most costly battles of the Pacific campaign of World War II – about 6,000 American marines died and 21,000 Japanese – and the Pacific battle off Midway Island is one of the most famous naval battles in history). "The world tilts. . . . I offer this votive candle to the God of Oki. . . ." (Oki Islands are a group of small Japanese islands in the southern part of the Sea of Japan.) "War is the dripping of blood. . . . From Oki, let us find a favorable wind with one thousand days of sunshine and peace."

LA ARGENTINA SHO (ADMIRING LA ARGENTINA, 1977)

By the time of Ohno Kazuo's famous dance *Admiring La Argentina*, Hijikata was defining himself more as a choreographer and director than a performer. In November of 1977, Ohno premiers *Admiring La Argentina*, directed by Hijikata Tatsumi at the *Dai-ichi Sei Mei* Hall, a dance for which he receives the Dance Critics' Circle Award. "Death and life in that order are the predominant themes in the opening scenes of *Admiring La Argentina*, in which Kazuo poignantly portrays Genet's prostitute's last moments" (Ohno and Ohno 2004: 76). Kazuo climbs onto the stage from the audience, leaving life behind, later to return to the same spot reborn as a young girl. Death in this dance unearths a more profound existence.

The performance of *Admiring La Argentina* serves as a rebirth for Ohno from the introspective 'death' during his ten-year absence from dance and the stage. He is seventy-one years old. The entire performance is a tribute to Mercé Antonia, a Spanish dancer known as La Argentina whom he had seen dance fifty years earlier. The only full-length videotape of the performance is in the Ohno Archives in Yokohama, which is not yet open to the public. In addition to a few film clips in collections of Ohno's works (Ohno 2001), written accounts describe it as a two-part performance, *Self-Portrait* and *La Argentina* (Ohno and Ohno 2004: 150–69). *Self-Portrait*, a series of four scenes, symbolizes the cycle of life of Ohno Kazuo. In "Divine's Death," he portrays a dying male prostitute inspired by Genet's character, *Divine*. Walking from a seat in the audience and up the aisle, he climbs the stairs to sink to the stage floor as he dies in deep suffering. In "Rebirth of a Young Girl," Ohno, now wearing a white chemise with a paper flower in his hair, appears after a brief blackout at the spot where the prostitute died. In the third scene "Daily Bread," he is clad in black trunks, appearing as himself in a physical expression of the body. In "The Marriage of Heaven and Earth," the final scene of the first act, Ohno stands, still wearing the black trunks, "crucified" against a grand piano, head thrown back and arms outstretched. This series of dances deals with death and rebirth and the nourishment of spiritual needs.

In the second act, the two scenes of "Flower and Bird" open with tango music. Ohno evokes the spirit of *La Argentina*: dancing in a dark green dress, changing to a flowing gown, and finally into a white ruffled

Figure 3.4

Ohno tossing back his head in *La Argentina sho* (Admiring La Argentina, 1977). Photograph by Ikegami Naoya. Courtesy Ohno Kazuo Archive

gown. In contrast to Western stage and drama in which a man wearing a dress potentially denotes cross-dressing, Ohno is not conscious that he is dressed as a woman. A metamorphosis takes place in which Argentina takes bodily form in his dance. Ohno and Argentina merge until Ohno becomes La Argentina. He offers homage to Argentina by sharing his experience of her through his embodiment of her; that is, he dances for her and with her.

Yoshito looks back on the events that caused Ohno to break out of his introspective phase through his reconnection with Argentina. In the interview below with Tamah Nakamura, March 19, 2005 in Yokohama, Yoshito describes this period of discovery:

Discovering Argentina:

For about ten years it was difficult for Kazuo to be on stage. He continued to get experience at small places and he taught Hijikata's students for two years or so at Hijikata's request. After that Kazuo made three movies in about four years. We, his family, didn't know what he was doing. He sometimes disappeared somewhere. I knew he was making movies but I really didn't know where he was making movies or what he was doing. He even shot a movie near here. When I look back, I think he was looking again at what he was through those movies. He was reflecting on his origin. He really looked at himself closely – even to the point of being with pigs and being smeared with dirt.

One day when he went to an art exhibition, he was so excited: "I saw Argentina," he said. I asked him: "What is Argentina?" He explained that he had seen Argentina, a Spanish dancer, when he was young, and that he saw her again today. "I was so moved," He said aloud: "Maybe I can dance." The picture he saw wasn't a photograph or a painted picture of the image of a woman. It was almost milky white and not much was painted clearly. *(The picture was an abstract painting of geometrical curves painted on a zinc sheet by Nakanishi Natsuyuki.)* It looked like a cow or like a bull fighting. There was almost nothing literally drawn in the picture. It was very wondrous. Certainly I could see how Kazuo recalled Argentina, when I saw the picture.

Two or three days after he saw Argentina at the art museum, Kazuo received various books on Argentina from Eiko and Koma, dancers and his students in New York. He was surprised and got so excited. He said he wanted to produce a stage performance. I asked him, "What kind of music did she dance to?" He said, "Well, she danced with modern music of that time." But there was no information left, and we had no idea what kind of music it was. Since she was born in Argentina, in Buenos Aires, she was called Argentina. She was originally from Spain and was named Antonia Mercé, so she went back to Spain and became a dancer. Since she was born in Argentina, we decided to dance with Argentine Tango. There was the most famous Argentine tango musician, Hayakawa Shinpei and his wife was Fujisawa Ranko. I looked for him, and finally found his apartment. "Well, Ohno-san," he said, " I am sorry but I no longer play. Argentine Tango requires a very high level of technique and skill." So I asked him, "Well Sensei, I believe you have something like records." He said, "I got rid of them all, but I will introduce you to one of my students, Ikeda." Ikeda was with a student band and performing at a festival. I asked him to come to our place and see my father's dance. After seeing my father's dance, Ikeda said, "I will do my best to play music for you; I really want to."

It was a few years before the 200th anniversary celebration of tango that Ohno performed Argentina. I think that was good timing, because if it had been later after tango got popular again, we could not have used tango for the Argentina performance. La Argentina was unique, since no one was using tango music at that time.

The performance of *Admiring La Argentina* is a pivotal stage for Ohno and for butoh for several reasons. It heralds the return to dancing and stage performance for Ohno after a hiatus of ten years of self-imposed reflection. Perhaps more significantly, the performance highlights Ohno as a star solo dancer. Further, the *La Argentina* performance creates a new relationship between Ohno and Hijikata, with Hijikata in a non-performance, advisory capacity. This new collaboration ensures the longevity of butoh beyond the earlier *Dance Experience* works, which could not be reproduced and restaged through the creation of deliberately structured forms. In a global perspective, from this period onward, Ohno's international repertoire grows extensively through restaging of his performances beyond Japan to twenty-nine countries. His successful performance of *La Argentina* at the Nancy Festival, France in 1980 launches his dance worldwide.

From there Argentina is reborn in Yokohama: A young Brazilian modern dancer, Antonio Fuerio, saw Ohno dance at the Nancy Festival. He was greatly impressed with Ohno's butoh rendition of *La Argentina*. Subsequently, he choreographed *Carmen Miranda: Homage to Kazuo Ohno* with his dance troupe, *Grupo de Teatro Macunaima* and performed it in March of 2005 in Yokohama, Japan. Fuerio's homage performance conjures a Brazilian Ohno dressed in a white suit with red rose in pocket, white bow tie, straw hat with black band – and a searching, wistful, soul.

There is an interesting historical trace here: In the beginning, Ohno's memory of Merce Antonia's performance was a catalyst fifty years later for his *Admiring La Argentina* performance in Nancy, France. Ohno's dance had lived in Fuerio's memory for twenty-five years when he brought his *Homage to Ohno* back to Yokohama, Japan from Brazil. In *Admiring La Argentina*, Ohno Kazuo built an international bridge through the feet of three dancers from two different world climates, combining the cool temperament of Japan with the heat of Argentina and Brazil.

SUIREN (WATER LILIES, 1987)

(In this section, we refer to the two Ohnos of *Water Lilies*, Kazuo and Yoshito, using their first names to avoid confusion.)

Kazuo's performances, nuanced through a conscious construction of his dancing body, are also true to his natural body – large hands, expressive face, and limberness. He is aware, as his son Yoshito says, of eyes all over his body, and the expressive power of the back of the body, never dissociating the front and the back (Ohno and Ohno 2004: 37–40). Nowhere is this integral sense of the dancing body more evident than in Kazuo's duet with Yoshito – *Suiren* (Water Lilies, 1987) – based on Claude Monet's *Water Lilies*, forty-eight highly successful landscape paintings the French impressionist artist explored from 1897 to 1900 and painted between 1904 and 1906. As in *La Argentina*, Kazuo draws inspiration from sources outside his native Japan, using images of great power and beauty to position the themes and characteristics of his dance. Behind *Suiren*, one senses the transparency and spiritual luminosity of Monet's work, the surface of the water, motionless or gently rippling, emerging through the flat leaves of the Water Lilies, and floating flowers in repose like the lotus lilies of Buddhist tranquility.

Kazuo, like Monet, gives the illusion of movement through calm and serenity, cultivating a feminine presence that one also finds in Monet, especially his reflective handling of water and light in his exquisite waterlily paintings. Kazuo's suave, flowing lines in *Suiren* remind us that Monet is one of the impressionist painters strongly influenced by the Japanese masters of Ukiyo-e, also called "Pictures of the Floating World" (Fraleigh 1999: 9–11). In choosing Monet, Kazuo incorporates a part of Japan's aesthetic history, whether consciously or not. (We explained the influence of Japanese Ukiyo-e on the French Impressionists in Chapter 1.) Monet's idea for painting varied images of his pond garden

Figure 3.5 Ohno in the first section of *Suiren* (Water Lilies, 1987)
Courtesy Ohno Kazuo Archive

at Giverny in several temporal planes came through Hokusai's *Hundred Views of Mount Fuji* and Hiroshige's *Hundred Views of Edo*. He saw these works at Samuel Bing's Paris gallery in 1888 and at the *Exposition Universelle* in 1889. Eventually Monet collected Ukiyo-e colored woodcut prints by Hokusai, Hiroshige, and Utamaro, some of which were displayed in the dining room of his home at Giverny, a small village northwest of Paris (Sagner-Duchting 1999: 34).

Hokusai foreshadowed impressionism at its source: part of Monet's inspiration for the Water Lily paintings (dating from about 1897) came from Hokusai's detailed woodcut *Chrysanthemum and Bee* that he had owned since 1896 (Ibid. 57). Monet's work marked impressionism as an aesthetic movement, and it borrowed liberally from the artistry of Japan. In time, Monet's friendly relations with Japanese art collectors and dealers Hayashi Tadamasu and Matsukata Kojiro who admired his work and introduced it to Japan, aided the symbiosis of Ukiyo-e and impressionist painting (Ibid. 34).

Kazuo problematizes impressionism and the great canvases of Monet in *Suiren;* he is not simply imitating them. In Monet's original paintings, flowers and leaves appear on reflecting water as viewed from above (like Ukiyo-e without horizon, and seemingly without limits), showing different seasons of the year and times of day in his garden under a Japanese bridge. Monet's cool and soothing scenes are devoid of people, and in their idealization of nature, cut off from narrative human themes. His is a beautiful, uninterrupted vision of warm, marshy, undisturbed water, with flowers symbolic of feminine fertility and interiors of the soul. Kazuo departs from the idealized surface of Monet and also from the illusions of French Impressionism in his juxtaposition of Yoshito with his own luminous dances in *Suiren*, telescoping him away from the shimmering surface, as though focused intensively through a broken mirror. Even as Kazuo's dances can elevate nature in the same open indeterminate way as Monet, they also break the static surface of contemplative perception, moving in the dark and messy places that trouble still waters.

Yoshito and Kazuo both transform thematically in this dance, moving neither without horizon nor along parallel lines, but together and apart, alive to their separate spheres. As in Kazuo's works in general, everything is alive to the moment, and each moment is an opportunity to peek through to another reality, to dream and reflect, yes, but also to grieve and change. Yoshito says of dancing with his father that as a twosome they transcend their separate identities and opposite approaches to performance, merging into a larger whole, even while maintaining separate voices (Ohno and Ohno 2004: 96). As in much butoh, white make up assists the blend. In *Suiren*, Kazuo and Yoshito wear *shiro-nuri*, the typical white make up of butoh, to erase individual personality and private history. Kazuo also applies thick black eye liner to accentuate his eyes. Indeed, he seems to use make up for both illusion and disappearance of personal features, so that his dance becomes more numinous, allowing a wide identification with the audience. He can be a woman in a frilly gown, as he is in the beginning of *Suiren*, or an old man leaning on a crooked stick trailing a long yellow kimono, a character he develops through the middle of the dance. Wearing the same white face with exaggerated eyes, he can also morph into more robust figures as he does at the end of *Suiren*, dancing in Western black formal attire, casually, the white shirt unbuttoned at the top, with his arms and hands telling short stories, summarizing life (as a pond) in transition.

Less flowering than Kazuo, Yoshito begins the dance as a blocky, tightly strung man in a suit. For a long time, he seethes inwardly with just a veneer of visible shaking, eventually exploding in short violent jump-starts that settle quickly back into taut oblivion. Yoshito holds an electric charge in this opening scene that these authors have seldom seen in theater, completely focused, percussively broken and riveting, and with such minimal means. Kazuo enters the stage quite unobtrusively in the beginning, almost like a whisper. The light gradually picks up his delicate, slowly moving presence and the gently ruffled gown that he wears as a second skin. He carries a parasol, sweetly feminine and old-fashioned, like the ones women in southern Japan use to block the sun on hot days, or the ones Monet used to protect his out-of-doors paintings at Giverny.

Kazuo inches along, his large eyes shining with tenderness in the glow of his white face. He captures our gaze from the beginning, like the exaggerated eyes and aging beauty of American movie icon Gloria Swanson whom Kazuo admired. The stark contrast between Kazuo and Yoshito opens a space in the mind, readying it for another condition.

The audience is invited to share in the flowering metamorphosis of the dance as it develops. Yoshito tells us that in Kazuo's world, flowers are cited as the most ideal form of existence; his physical presence must at all times be flowerlike (Ohno and Ohno 2004: 89). *Suiren* invites us to join Kazuo's world in this respect, finally making an explicit identification with nature. Kazuo's use of flowers appeared early on in his 1981 work *My Mother*. Yoshito comments on Kazuo's embodiment of flowers:

> By becoming an integral part of the body's nervous system, a flower functions much in the same way an insect's antennae do: constantly palpating the air. Not only does it receive and respond to incoming stimuli, it also acts as a natural extension of the hand, and, in doing so, becomes a point of contact with the outside world. It functions independently as though it were an external eye detached from the trunk of the body. In that respect it exists both as an autonomous entity and as a sensory organ.
>
> (Ibid.)

As a metamorphic signature dance of Kazuo with his son Yoshito, *Suiren* shifts magically through several stages (or canvases) from its opening scene, juxtaposing Kazuo's extended entrance in a fragile gown with Yoshito dancing to the music of *Pink Floyd* in his blocky-man suit. In view of the dance's impressionistic pulse, this is the pond as cosmos, seen in the dawning light (Kazuo) and shattering surfaces (Yoshito) of morning. The light fades up to midday, featuring Kazuo's solo in a long yellow kimono at the pond's zenith. Here he dances in glowing gestures that eventually wane, as he trails the kimono behind his almost nude and aging body, and leans on his gnarled walking staff through various incarnations. The dance gradually gathers an evening atmosphere, the pond at twilight and the birth of Yoshito as a White Lotus Goddess in a long white robe, crowned with a magnificent Buddhist lotus, also a lily. In the chakra system of Asian yoga, the lotus opens the seventh energy system of the body at the crown of the head, extending the body into pure spirit.

It would, however, be trite and predictable to finish with this climax, and Kazuo, ever unpredictable, seeks another end, one more earthy in his black suit and white shirt, even casually postmodern, meeting us where we are for the night, settled there in our own black attire, or blue jeans, while he communicates not of other worlds but of this one here and now tonight, his gestures drawing us intimately into the enclosure of his storied hands. When he bows, we get this message over again, as he embraces us whole in one flowing movement that gathers in the heart chakra. No wonder there are few dry eyes. Kazuo, as many audiences around the world know, can make you cry.

INTERVIEW WITH YOSHITO OHNO – ON *SUIREN* – TAMAH NAKAMURA, MARCH 19, 2005

Tamah: What is your memory of dancing with your father in *Suiren*?

Yoshito: This was Kazuo's first work after Hijikata's death. I performed *Suiren* with my father at the opening of a drama festival in Stuttgart, Germany. This was its first performance. On our return to Japan, we performed *Suiren* for the butoh festival held in *Ginza* in Tokyo.

Tamah: It was the first performance without Hijikata.

Yoshito: Yes, that's right.

Tamah: How did that affect your performance?

Yoshito: Since we had depended pretty much on Hijikata, I was worried at that time and felt insecure. Well, I was very worried, but in Stuttgart there was a large party hosted by the drama festival after the performance.

Tamah: Ohno-sensei is very international!

Yoshito: Yes, people were pleased with the performance very much. And when the first performance was held at *Saison* in *Ginza*, Hijikata's friend, Minoru Yoshioka-sensei, at a party after the performance praised the performance highly. His wife also said to me, "You did an amazing thing." I was surprised; it made me feel I wanted to continue to perform from that moment on. She encouraged me very much.

Tamah: Did you and Kazuo make *Suiren* between the two of you?

Yoshito: Together. Yes.

Tamah: In *Suiren* you also danced with your father as an equal for the first time.

Yoshito: Yes, that's right. That was the first time I had to create my own part. It was an awesome experience. I was really worried and didn't know what to dance until the last minute.

Tamah: What were the connections between you and Kazuo afterwards?

Yoshito: Well, the core work in *Suiren*, "Portrait," the scene of "Portrait," ah, in that I danced my own dance and Kazuo did the dance he created. But I felt something was missing, something that connected my dance and Kazuo's with Hijikata. I thought we needed one, just one water lily to give to Hijikata. That's the most important thing. When we thought of that we were connected. Our minds bonded. At that time, Kazuo was still dancing, but now I have to dance for Hijikata. I want to dance and give one flower to Hijikata. I still have that thought now that he is gone. But it has not been achieved yet. It is not easy.

THE FUTURE OF BUTOH

Dance forms, to survive, must change and evolve in new contexts. Definitions of dance, as of art in general, are temporal and situated; they also evolve. Some of the institutions and activities available in Japan for advancing understanding of butoh through Hijikata and Ohno are: the Taro Okamoto Museum of Art, Kawasaki City with its *2003 Exhibition of "Tatsumi Hijikata's Butoh"*; the Keio Art Center Hijikata Archive, Keio University, Tokyo; the Ohno Dance Studio Archives, Yokohama, a private collection on Ohno, seeking an exhibition home; and an academic project in process at the Hijikata Archive to do an extensive evaluation of Hijikata's *butoh-fu*, sixteen bound scrapbooks of collections of his writings and images for dances from the early 1970s to 1985.

4

DANCE EXPERIENCES

INTRODUCTION TO METAMORPHIC EXPLORATIONS

This chapter invites students and teachers to experience selected butoh practices. Hijikata and Ohno identified their work as *dance experience* first of all. Hijikata Tatsumi DANCE EXPERIENCE *no kai* (Hijikata Tatsumi's Dance Experience Meeting) was the title for Hijikata's first dance recital in July of 1960. The title with English in all capital letters defines from the beginning his approach of direct experience. As in a ritual, the dancer and audience transform through the experience of the event. Thus DANCE EXPERIENCE is an approach for butoh practice and a definition of dance as close to the body, a personal experience not accessible through mere observation or interpretation. In this sense butoh is a somatic study, since somatics is concerned primarily with first person experience – how you perceive your body-self in changing states of being – not what others see. When butoh involves an audience, it aims to share interpersonal experience.

The text introduces DANCE EXPERIENCES from nine prominent butoh performers and teachers. We present these experiences as "metamorphic explorations," because they pass from one state to another in transformational modes characteristic of butoh. We acknowledge that dance cannot be learned from a text, and serious students of butoh need to learn from an experienced teacher and proponent of this form, perhaps even a *guru* as understood in the East, the teacher who opens your heart. The workshop words of the butoh teachers we include are intended to augment butoh practice, not to replace the teacher. They are put forth in the spirit of sharing the experiential butoh legacy, and present selected butoh methods and processes with supporting aesthetic theories that extend back to Hijikata and Ohno. Most articles and books on butoh are historical or aesthetic, and do not deal with butoh as practice. We are interested in opening up dialogue and research in this area. DANCE EXPERIENCE explorations are selected, edited, and constructed in light of *practice as research*.

Workshop words and DANCE EXPERIENCES of Nakajima Natsu who studied with Hijikata are represented here, as are those of Ohno Kazuo's son, Ohno Yoshito, who danced with his father and Hijikata throughout the entire development of butoh. We note that Yoshito still teaches explorations evolved by his father in their studio in Yokohama. Harada Nobuo, a second-generation butoh dancer, is also a contributor – as are Takenouchi Atsushi, Morita Itto, Takeuchi Mika, Yoshioka Yumiko, and British dancer Frances Barbe, third-generation butoh performers who ground their work in the original techniques of Hijikata and Ohno while offering individual innovations. In addition, we comment on Waguri Yukio's (1998) CD-Rom of Hijikata's *butoh-fu*. Waguri is one of Hijikata's original students, and his CD-Rom presents important research into Hijikata's dance notation, teaching, and the performance of butoh. Authors Sondra Fraleigh and Tamah Nakamura have taken workshops at Ohno's studio in Yokohama, Fraleigh with Kazuo and Nakamura with Yoshito. Fraleigh has also taken workshops with Waguri, Nakajima, Yoshioka, Ashikawa Yoko, Kasai Akira, Endo Tadashi, and American butoh teachers, Lani Weissbach, and Joan Laage (Laage studied with Ohno Kazuo and Ashikawa Yoko). Nakamura has also studied extensively with Harada Nobuo. Thus the authors' experiences of butoh also inform this chapter. Where the authors have extended DANCE EXPERIENCES to address them directly to the reader, this is clearly marked.

First we summarize guiding concepts in the development and practice of butoh. Some of the points have been made already in other contexts, but they bear repeating here. The following pairs show aesthetic propensities on the left with correlating themes on the right.

1   Darkness – Spirit
2   Metamorphosis – Shapeshifting

These terms come up in various ways in the following explorations.

NOTE TO TEACHERS

If you want to include any of the DANCE EXPERIENCES in your work with others, please take time to experience them for yourself first. Become a student, and practice mindfully. Spend time reflecting on the dance/life process involved, so you can embody the explorations and let them shine through your own words. Keep a journal of your DANCE EXPERIENCES. Please acknowledge the source of any exploration you use in your teaching.

NOTE TO STUDENTS

DANCE EXPERIENCES presented here can be a springboard for personal development, dance improvisations, and choreography; they also lead into butoh-influenced performance. Most of the explorations are improvisational and will change, as will you, each time you do them. Do the ones that appeal to you more than once, so you can appreciate how time and circumstance play a role in your awareness, as in your life and dances. Don't judge the results of your performance; just become a witness to yourself in transformation.

NOTE ON JOURNALING

Keep a journal of your DANCE EXPERIENCES. In the spirit of *butoh-fu*, you might want to extend this journal into a scrapbook full of your words, poems, drawings, photographs, or even cutout pictures that stir something in you. Consider how you want to juxtapose word and pictorial images. What do you want to call your journal?

NOTE ON DARKNESS

Darkness is the word that more than any other has become synonymous with butoh. We have spoken of darkness in various ways throughout the text, and emphasized its spiritual dimensions in Chapter 2 (see especially, "Spiritual Darkness: Inside Ohno's Studio and *Konpaku*"). Inspiration for butoh can come from anywhere; we know that Christianity affected Ohno as much as Buddhism did, and Hijikata asserted that his dance did not come from religion, but from the mud. Students do not need to adopt a religious perspective to experience butoh. Butoh relates to the spirituality of the body itself, as something all humans possess. Darkness in butoh has nothing to do with evil, but refers to the spirituality that is mythically associated with feminine principles of softness, earth, and surrender of ego, as Nakajima makes clear in her speech and article on *Ankoku Butoh* and Feminine Spirituality (1997). For students interested in pursuing this perspective further, *Dancing Identity* provides an extended metaphysical revaluing of darkness (Fraleigh 2004).

NOTE ON COOKING

Ohno taught life/death/life cycles as the basis of butoh. We are reminded by butohist Endo Tadashi, who collaborated with Ohno Kazuo, that like cooking, butoh is not separate from life processes. Endo talks about selecting the best foods, looking for fresh ingredients, color, and interesting shapes for cooking, and how it is the same in dancing. Dancers themselves should be fresh, which doesn't have anything to do with age, he says, but with how the dancer approaches the dance (Daiwa International Butoh Festival in London UK, Symposium October 9, 2005). He also says that just as you would never serve poor food to guests, you want to give your best performances to audiences. Since 1992, Endo has been director of the Butoh-Centre MAMU in Göttingen, Germany. His butoh stems from *Ma*, a Japanese word that indicates being "in between." His workshops offer both the experience of Japanese Butoh and explorations of your own individual dance.

NOTE ON EMPTINESS AND EMERGENCE

Endo tells us to remember that there is nothing intentionally expressed in butoh; rather does the butoh dancer exist on the edges of time, holding a secret inside, emptiness, waiting to emerge (Endo's butoh workshop in London UK, October 2, 2005). Bear this in mind, and be prepared to surprise yourself, as you hear the *Workshop Words* and explore *DANCE EXPERIENCES* of several contemporary butohists in the following sections.

NAKAJIMA NATSU: BECOMING NOTHING/ BECOMING SOMETHING

Nakajima Natsu is an amazing female butohist who introduced her own choreographic visions in highly technical total theater events to multinational audiences on several world tours. She still teaches and performs butoh, and uses it to work with handicapped people and in dance therapy settings. As one of the original students and associates of both Hijikata and Ohno, Nakajima explains that through butoh she "borrowed the field of the body" to go on a spiritual journey (Nakajima 1997: 3).

Nakajima's workshop words on Becoming Nothing

We begin with *Becoming Nothing/Becoming Something* through workshop words from Nakajima that originated in the approach of Hijikata. Sondra Fraleigh first experienced this meditative and metamorphic exploration through Nakajima's teaching in Toronto in 1988, and wrote extensively about it in her book on Butoh, Zen, and Japan (Fraleigh 1999: 87–96). She reconstructs it again here with added commentary from Nakajima.

DANCE EXPERIENCE

When she begins a class, Nakajima often warms-up the students in a short free form improvisation to music, encouraging students in the words of Hijikata to "shed the skin of the body that has been tamed and domesticated."

Warm up

➤ Improvise freely. Use music that has drive and rhythm, anything to get you moving, as you play with the feelings that arise and follow your intuition. Track down signs of habit in your body. How can you explore more of your potential to move freely?

➤ Let go of the look of your body, and become more aware of how your movement feels.

➤ Hijikata was "like a spy" Nakajima says – "tracking down all the signs of domestication of the body." Shedding the social body is essential to Ankoku Butoh and to "the body that becomes nothing."

Disappearance

➤ Start at one end of the studio and begin an extended moving meditation on disappearance (about 20 minutes). Use soft music

Figure 4.1 Nakajima Natsu in "Stone Play" from her full-length concert work –
Sleep and Reincarnation from Empty Land (1989). Photograph by
Nourit Masson-Sekine

of the Japanese harp in the background or a Shakuhachi flute (traditional Japanese flute music). Lower your center of gravity and slightly bend your knees, as you walk toward the other end of the studio in the now famous butoh manner of hokohtai (the walking body). Sense your weight sinking through your feet and into the floor. Sense the spine lengthening, and allow there to be softness in the chest. Don't collapse it, nor push it out, just allow softness to be there.

➤ There is an amorphous form for this slow sinking walk of *hokohtai*, but it can vary according to your feeling at the moment. Allow your dance to unfold gently, smoothly by sliding your feet along the floor with steps no longer than the size of your own foot. You can make the stops slightly smaller, or maybe even a little larger if you need to for balance.

➤ Let your arms hang easily at your sides without dangling. Remember these are your arms; sense their ease, their aliveness. Do they float ever so slightly away from your body as you lower your center of gravity?

➤ Place an imaginary plate of water on your head as you lower your center, and move smoothly so as not to spill the water – or break the spell created by the walking. Let your eyes become soft also, as they move further into oblivion. Sense eyes around you, as part of you, all over you.

➤ If you are moving in a group, experience how you move as one, and individual egos disperse, palpably, into the atmosphere.

➤ Carry eternity with you, and your ancestors. Walk to the other side of the room as you ask your body to disappear. Eventually forget to ask, and just disappear. Nothing to think. Nothing to do. Become nothing.

Reappearance

➤ When you reach the other side of the room (about a 20 minute process of shedding your body), turn around simply, still in the same walking posture, moving forever on in your meditative gait (another 20 minutes, approximately). Continue the walking, gradually, sensing the return of your flesh and bones. Not "doing" anything, simply walking back over the same space as you return.

➤ Be patient. Take your time, and without trying, allow any change that wants to come from within your body to occur.

➤ Is there a secret waiting in you to emerge? If there is, let it take any shape it wants to. Let your consciousness move and melt as it will, and your body find where it wants to stop.

Preparing to Disappear and Reappear with butoh-fu and workshop words of Nakajima

➤ Before you take the butoh journey described above, you can prepare with *butoh-fu* from Hijikata that Nakajima sometimes uses in her workshops: "There is a third eye in the middle of your forehead ..." Nakajima says. I think of this as the third eye of yoga just between my eyes, also called "the blue pearl of bliss," and the seat of vision and consciousness. I let my own awareness develop peacefully by closing and relaxing my eyes before beginning the movement meditation. Nakajima would prompt you into that eye as you become nothing, and bit-by-bit begin to disappear.

➤ When she teaches, she quotes more *butoh-fu* metaphors from Hijikata, and spaces them out in the time of disappearing. If you want to prepare the DANCE EXPERIENCE of "Becoming Nothing" through *butoh-fu* inspired by Hijikata and quoted by Nakajima, use the following:

> *Butoh is the walk of smoke ... because Butoh is about disappearing, that is why a form is left behind ... The disappearing history of the flesh trails behind the metropolis of the flesh ... In our body, there is something that sometimes goes astray, and sometimes surfaces...*

(Nakajima 1997: 7)

➤ Write this *butoh-fu* down before doing the exploration, and spend some time preparing your awareness with it as you also cultivate your third eye. Ohno uses a similar process, looking at pictures and reading his own butoh-fu to peak his awareness before dancing, then letting go of this preparation to allow spontaneity in performance, as we took up toward the end of Chapter 2.

➤ You can practice the slow smooth walk of *hokohtai* by balancing a light-weight bamboo stalk (pole) on your head as you lower your center of gravity by slightly bending the knees. It seems a little shaky at first, but you will be surprised how quickly you can learn this balance with a little practice.

Fraleigh's reflection

Becoming Nothing and Becoming Something is a profoundly spiritual and meditative exploration that exposes a basic tenet of butoh. Namely: that each person in his or her own way can assimilate DANCE EXPERIENCES. This one is about treading a lifeline to the meeting place of life and death as Ohno taught. Dancers often burst into tears and are cleansed by what Nakajima calls "the return to the original body." I remember this still when I'm walking sometimes with no place to go, and capture a short haiku:

> Trailing my body
> In amazement, I walk
> Into stillness awake

Nakajima's reflection

The first step, toward spiritual awareness through butoh, Nakajima explains, is "to shed the things that are daily and social, to return to the original body." In Hijikata's words, to become "a body as a corpse." The original body belongs to all traditional Japanese performing arts, Nakajima emphasizes. Noh performers take ten years to achieve such an objective. Western dance techniques in contrast, emphasize the visual world of constructed appearance. "To return to the original body" is an invisible technique. This is essential so that dance may surge from the depths of the body (nature, spirit, and the unconscious). Nakajima puts it this way:

> In Ankoku Butoh, "something moves, something dances"; it is not the individual human being who moves or dances.

This condition of *Becoming Nothing*, Nakajima says, is not really a condition of emptiness, but is actually a "filled emptiness" ready to morph to another dimension. She explains in terms of her own dancing:

> When I dance ... the movements germinate in the deep centre of my body, and my body *is moved*.

> (Ibid. 8)

NOTE ON *BUTOH-FU* AND CHOREOGRAPHY

In the latter part of his life, Hijikata took up the challenge of trying to create form (*Something*) by creating a dance notation, his *butoh-fu*, as we explained in Chapter 2. Nakajima provides a concrete example in the following. She sometimes teaches Hijikata's choreography for this *butoh-fu*, seeking, like an investigative detective or phenomenologist to explain the world of appearance – *Becoming Something*. Nakajima teaches the following *butoh-fu* as movements explicitly choreographed by Hijikata. Thus we understand that *butoh-fu* are not always improvised. They can be strictly choreographed in fine detail as Hijikata did, even as they also involve the dancer in metamorphic transformations. Through compelling, ever-changing landscapes of the human face, strange transitions (transmogrification) become important toward the end of Nakajima's dance. Here are Hijikata's *butoh-fu*:

long pipe
combing
resting chin on the table
tying a knot in the string
stretching the string
carrying a cup
weaving cherry blossom branches
hair ornament
lipstick
stop!
cutting the string with teeth
stretching the string
outline of your face
loose hair
big nose
three streams of rain crossing in front of your face three times
TOKIWA [a beautiful lady of legend in Japan]
Ogress

Nakajima's rendition of this *butoh-fu* in her work Niwa (The Garden, premiered in Tokyo in 1982) demonstrates the power of Hijikata's storied world and shapeshifting, as she morphs from a young and beautiful woman to an old hag. Watching her, one sees that her condition is spiritually alive, especially in her face, and that her face might dissolve its dance or reverse at any moment.

DANCE EXPERIENCE

Choreographic instructions by Sondra Fraleigh, inspired by Nakajima's *Niwa*

The face of deconstruction and transmogrification

I know "transmogrification" is a big word, but it's also very evocative, and refers to compelling, even grotesque, transformations (as noted above). When the face becomes the focus of attention in dance and theater, it can seem strangely other, like a mask that can move and morph. Let the fascinating strangeness of your face emerge in this exploration.

➤ Begin by making a list of about 18 words or word clusters that are as evocative (and mundane) as Hijikata's *butoh-fu* above, not concerning yourself with how they will connect. Make the last two words highly contrasting, or opposite. Choreograph a short dance phrase for each word or cluster and memorize it in detail. The phrases might begin with gestures of the face, hands, or feet, but let them resonate throughout the body.

➤ Now connect these memorized phrases, and see how your face enters into the dance of the whole. Let your face reflect the *butoh-fu* you have made for your choreography. This DANCE EXPERIENCE is not about making faces, but about allowing the dance of the face to emerge. The facial contours and feelings might be very large at times or so subtle as to barely be noticed. Memorize and practice the face along with the whole dance, but consider that it is constantly in transition and never held.

➤ Now deconstruct the dance by taking away everything but the echo of the words that have entered into the dance of your face. Keep the dance of your face alive, and be brave enough to let go of the hard work you put into making the gestures. Maybe you can save what you have learned in making the gestures and phrases for another dance – but for now, EXPERIENCE the pure dance of your face.

➤ Give your dance a name. Perform it for someone you trust not to judge it, someone who will enter into the spirit of the dance of your face with you. Or maybe you will perform it for an audience, as a work on its own, or a section of a dance work. It doesn't have to be called butoh. That can be your secret. Greg Hicks of the Royal Shakespeare Company uses butoh techniques for his performance of the Ghost in Hamlet, the secret of his standard-setting performance. (He told this secret when on a panel at the Daiwa International Butoh Festival in London, 2005).

Time

➤ The deconstructive choreographic process outlined above can't be accomplished in a single rehearsal or compositional session. Plan several hours within the space of about three weeks for this DANCE EXPERIENCE, depending on how many words you use.

➤ Allow time to truly memorize your phrases and choreograph them in detail. Then you will need time to remove the choreography, allowing the face to remain as an echo – or we might say in butoh – *the body that becomes*.

A question?

➤ If you would like a Zen question to meditate on as you prepare this dance, use this one: What was my original face?

OHNO YOSHITO: THE PATIENCE OF NOT STARTING (*KONKI NO IRU MISHUPPATSU*)

In a workshop that Tamah Nakamura took from Ohno Yoshito in Yokohama, Japan in March of 2005, he used the following *butoh-fu* typical of his father's approach to teaching. Students may want to write this down as a meditative visualization, and four line haiku, in preparation for the following dance experiences on "The Patience of Not Starting."

The flower grows
The blossoms die
A bird takes wing nearby
And the wilting flower petals scatter

Yoshito, one of the major dancers of butoh, performed with his father in Japan and on his international tours for many years; he continues to take care of his father and serve his work as a teacher with Kazuo reaching his one-hundredth birthday in 2006. Most recently, when Kazuo dances in his wheelchair, Yoshito is nearby to transport him, to accompany and support his father in any way that is needed, and he takes care of him at home with the help of others. In Japan, parents, teachers, and the ancestors, hold a place of respect and honor, as Yoshito's life reflects.

Figure 4.2 Ohno Yoshito in *The Dead Sea* (1985). Photograph by Ikegami Naoya

He has mirrored and complemented his father's dance (in stark contrast sometimes) since his teen years when he began to dance with Hijikata and Kazuo in *Kinjiki*, the 1959 performance that marked the beginning of butoh.

Yoshito sometimes opens his workshops by showing an interconnected series of three watercolor prints in the book *Sotatsu* by Yamane Yuzo: 1) a water lily blossoms in a pond; 2) a bird takes flight; 3) water lily petals fall. He explains that butoh is like the poetic process in this painting:

> This water lily is a body and this bird is a kind of society. This is a tense relationship interacting in the air. *Sotatsu* painted that tense relationship between the pond and the bird 500 years ago. I think this is a scene of butoh.

Yoshito's workshop words on Patience

Yoshito's workshop words are recorded and translated by Tamah Nakamura, March 19, 2005. DANCE EXPERIENCES on the teaching of Yoshito are reconstructed and extended with preparations and further instructions by Fraleigh and Nakamura.

Note on Orchids, Patience, and *Shin*

In his workshops, Yoshito sometimes teaches "The Patience of Not Starting," taking this theme from the *shinpijimu* (Cymbidium), an orchid that takes seven years to grow starting from bacteria, from fungi. For Kazuo this *not starting* is the essence of butoh, according to Yoshito. He says that an important element of this is *shin* (centeredness, heart, body, tree trunk, spirit).

DANCE EXPERIENCE

Shin

➤ Begin by visualizing *Shin* – the very center of your body. This isn't a place; it is a feeling. Yoshito says that in Japanese *shin* is written as *kusa no kokoro* (heart of grass). Now begin to walk holding something. How slow is this walk – "the patience of not starting"? Yoshito says that "if you continue to walk for seven years, when the thing you are holding is gone you will have *shin* in yourself." He says "you need patience to reach what he calls *butoh*, and that just as Hijikata also danced with a flower in his hand, the flower is a butoh theme." Remember that Ohno had a special relationship to flowers, considering them "sensory organs." Yoshito says that flowers are the most ideal form of existence in Kazuo's world.

➤ Carry your flower in the center of your heart. Keep moving on with the flower, until you become the flower. As you transform into the flower, let your heart guide your dance. Carry patience in your heart, just as the flower is unassuming and gives its fragrance to the world without being asked. Let the flower carry you now. Let your dance finish in its own time and its own way. Continue to breathe into the *shin* of yourself. What is left residing in your body?

Preparation for Shin

➤ Write down Kazuo's *butoh-fu* haiku on flowers at the beginning of this section, so you can refer to it and let it ruminate in your dance. Find simple music that is soft and harmonious, that has fragrance and heart. Use instrumental music, not voice, because the words can interfere with your pure flower-consciousness. Spend time in nature looking at flowers, maybe a garden, or wildflowers in fields and beside the pavement. This might be a forgotten flower or one that is tended. Choose your flower. In your journal, paint or draw your flower as practice for the DANCE EXPERIENCE on *Shin*.

Reflections from Yoshito

In my first recital, when I was at the age of thirty, in 1969, I was practicing very hard and I asked Hijikata to write something about my dance. He said, OK, and he wrote: "Yoshito's dance is flower and bird." Anyone could see that, but he just wrote flower and bird. Well, they are internal and external elements tied together.

DANCE EXPERIENCE

Hair-split Difference (Kamihitoe)

When Yoshito teaches *Hair-split Difference*, he likes to show a poster of Hijikata hanging on the wall in which he is wearing a long dress and carrying a rose in front of him. He says that Hijikata walks with a flower wrapped in a tissue during practice so that he carries the flower with a thin layer of space between his hand and the flower creating softness in his center (*shin*). Yoshito describes that softness in *shin* as a "hair-split difference" (*Kamihitoe*):

It is just a hair-split difference. With that difference you can attract people's attention. Whether you have this small difference or not that makes a great difference. Hijikata practiced placing a piece of paper between his hands, like this: (Yoshito demonstrates by drawing one tissue from the box setting on the table. He allows the tissue to float to a resting position gently between the palms of his hands held in front of his chest.)

It will take a long time, but I hope you will acquire this form. You have to feel it in spirit. Quietness. As Basho's Poem *Shizukasa ya Iwa ni Shimi iru Semi no Koe* (The Cicada's Voice in the Quiet Rock): *There is truth even in the rock. And even the rock knows that.*

The Process

➤ Begin by placing a tissue under your arm (both arms) and hold your two hands in front of you, as you might in prayer. Leave just enough space to gently hold the tissue. That is how Kabuki actors walk like women (called *kamihikitori*) – with *one tissue space* between the arm and the side of the body.

➤ The softness of the one tissue space becomes part of your spirit and inner life as you move in minute increments across the studio floor for about twenty minutes practicing this exercise with soft music playing.

DANCE EXPERIENCE

Be a Stone

"When Ohno Kazuo visited Auschwitz," Yoshito tells us, "he found that he couldn't dance there. Then he saw some stones in the wall along the path he was walking and he could dance. He could dance the pain in the stones."

➤ Yoshito's only instructions for this exercise, as Nakamura experienced it, are to "be a stone." He says that there will be many kinds of stones in people. He tells us that Kazuo would say: "Don't think about being a stone; just find the stone in you."

➤ In the dance studio, search your body for your own stone to the sound of wind. Use a recording of wind sounds, or a score that features wind.

As an alternative to the studio experience, you might like to try this DANCE EXPERIENCE without recorded sound and out in the environment – in the presence of stones.

Preparation for "Be a Stone" (whether in the studio or natural environment)

➤ Find a place where you can be alone with stones, or relatively so. Stand on them. Feel them under your feet and on your skin. Pick them up, feel the various weights, textures, and see the colors.

➤ Never mind thinking too much about this; just experience the stones; be with them for a while before undertaking the DANCE EXPERIENCE.

➤ Feel the stillness in stones, or maybe you are attracted to the molecular movement inside, or how stones breathe and change with time.

➤ Reflect on yourself as stone.

➤ Experience age through the stones, as you connect to Ohno Kazuo's longevity, and remember he inspires this dance experience. He will be 100 years old in 2006, and Yoshito says there is nothing physically wrong with him, just weakness from old age. He dances from his wheelchair, and sometimes does a dance of struggle for uprightness from the floor. His arms waft and wink, and when he is relaxed in his dance, his face is soft and smiling. One doesn't see wrinkles when looking at Ohno, just light.

Nakamura's reflections

Nakamura describes her observations of DANCE EXPERIENCES on *Be a Stone*:

From my position sitting on the floor at the low table next to Kazuo's empty chair in the dance studio in Yokohama, I look out at the people *being a stone*. Desperately wringing an imaginary stone between the palms of his hands, a young man's grimace expresses the emotions dripping from the stone. A woman with her head flung back and her face looking up staggers forward with closed eyes and her arms hanging, carrying the heavy burden of her stone. A man jumps and lands on his feet, violently crashing his stone against unseen forces. A woman sits in a kneeling position piling up stones in front of her. I experience the energy of the stones as intensely alive and interactive

— searching for the living stone connects us to *the stone out there* in our environment and to *the world as stone.*

Fraleigh's reflections

I made this haiku poem, *Stone*, for my butoh journal immediately after taking a workshop with Ashikawa Yoko. I think of it as my personal definition of dance:

> Stone Still Body
> There is Nothing
> That is Not Moving

If you are keeping a DANCE EXPERIENCE journal or scrapbook, you might want to write your own haiku on *Be a Stone*. Write three short lines of around 17 syllables of 5/7/5. Haiku are generally three lines, but can vary according to the arrangement of the words, and 5/7/5 is just a guide, not a prescription. The important thing is to keep the poem short and whole. Hear the words. Don't edit them at first. Thoughtful shaping of the poem can come later. Keep it simple. Ohno wrote simple haiku as inspiration for dance, as we just saw and also considered in Chapter 2 in "Words that Dance: Ohno's Images."

YOSHIOKA YUMIKO: BODY RESONANCE

In 1994 butoh dancer Yoshioka Yumiko founded TEN PEN CHii art labor company with Joachim Manger, a visual artist from Germany. Their Schloss Broellin is an old castle in the countryside outside of Berlin, and the home of EXIT Dance Research and Exchange Project for summer study and performance of butoh and other projects. "Ten pen chii" means "natural catastrophe," originally "the sky (ten) changes and the earth (chi) changes." Yoshioka says that *everything is changing in connection. Our life consists of continuous interactions between nature, society, energy, and ourselves.* Early in her dance career, she performed with the female butoh company *Ariadone.* Now Yoshioka pioneers butoh installations with visual art and teaches her methods internationally. She believes in the necessity for human sharing of tasks and creative energy, and that butoh is a medium or catalyst to open human potential. Yoshioka's workshop words help illuminate the relationship between butoh and the method of Noguchi Michizo that we refer to in several places of this chapter. She contributes the following as an introduction to her method.

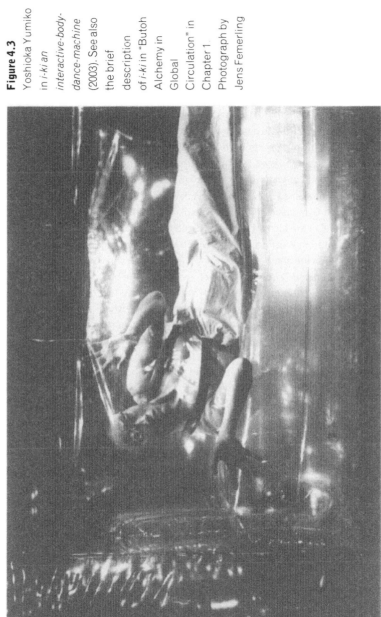

Figure 4.3
Yoshioka Yumiko in *i-ki* an *interactive-body-dance-machine* (2003). See also the brief description of *i-ki* in "Butoh Alchemy in Global Circulation" in Chapter 1. Photograph by Jens Femerling

Yoshioka's workshop words

I call my dance approach (or my body work) "Body Resonance." The world, including our body and soul, consists of vibrational waves that create constant resonances like echoes. When we tune our body to a certain frequency, we consequently get a resonance, and according to the frequency, we get different resonances. In order for this to happen, we need to first get rid of unnecessary tension. We make a white canvas of our body in order to paint new color on it. I teach this as neutralization, encouraging a close to a zero-state, scouring off rust and polishing antenna to catch waves from a profound layer of the body.

The image of water or air is easy to access, especially the idea that water can wash away extra tension. I developed this exercise mainly from Noguchi Gymnastics (Noguchi Taiso), which I learned in Japan. Yoga and Tai Chi are also influences. Noguchi Michizo's gymnastics is quite different from Western styles in which the main intention is to train and strengthen the body.

Like *Noguchi Taiso*, my approach focuses on the body's dialogue with gravity and integration of the body with image and feeling (the senses). My goal is not the training of muscles as in Western dance, but the refinement of the senses. To enjoy the process is more important than to gain Olympian technique. I also follow Noguchi in his research of the body in connection with Japanese language and ideograms, including the Chinese characters. He believed that both movement and language come from the body. In other words, the body is the root for both of them, and that is why it's difficult to translate Noguchi's work to foreign languages.

Many actors and dancers in Japan learn the simple but rich exercises of Noguchi to research and explore their body, soul, and mind. I practiced it when I was dancing butoh in *Ariadone Company* (Big Camel Battleship Company), but I started studying the essence of his method in 1993 through classes led by Noguchi himself, and I am still studying it in Tokyo with Terashima Yasuko, who is a prominent student of Noguchi. One of my basic explorations influenced by Noguchi is *Hanging Body (Water Bag)*. I teach this to introduce the feeling of the body's intrinsic connections.

DANCE EXPERIENCE

Yoshioka uses energizing music for this and motivates students with her zest for movement. Here are her instructions. They flow together in a single process for about 30 minutes. This can be an energizing warm up for later compositional work in butoh, or transformational butoh experiences.

Hanging Body (Water Bag)

Our bodies are water bags:

➤ As water bags, we are hanging from the thread connected to the center of the earth and the center of the sky.
➤ Let your water bag hang from a thread. Where is the thread? Is it tying the top of your head or your ear to the heavens, or your knee or elbow? Find out how your water bag hangs, and feel its connection to the earth through your feet.
➤ Shake the bag, or feel how somebody is shaking it.
➤ Reach up with your arms and then squat down in your water bag.
➤ Keep doing this until you feel a little tired.

Now take a minute to renew before continuing.

➤ Let the water flow and circulate, getting lukewarm so that the life can be born; then let a wave occur. Sense how your body is just part of a long transmitting wave. Make the wave in your own way, and allow energy to flow smoothly, giving and receiving, go back and forth for a while, then up and down. Give time to the wave in these directions.
➤ Then let the wave move through your sides and around.
➤ Circle your torso in a wave. How does this wave feel in your feet?
➤ Rest for a short time now – just long enough to feel a new direction begin.

Give wasted water weight back to the earth, and receive fresh water as we continue.

➤ Take time with this. Think of becoming transparent water or thick water like jelly. Play with these images of transparency and thickness.
➤ According to these images, your water bag changes. It is important not to fix the image in the body. Rather, the water is like a kaleidoscope, constantly changing. Think of action and reaction.

➤ Nothing can be done by force; just let it happen.

➤ At first, move consciously; then forget the movements as you let them happen automatically.

How is your water bag dancing now?

Yoshioka's words on Restricting the Frame

In my *Body Resonance Workshops*, I usually do relaxation exercises at first, then dynamic work to energize the body, which can also lead into transformational butoh work. For this, we need to expose certain tensions that can also restrict the frame of our body. I call it "freedom in unfreedom," or "freedom in restriction." The restriction is very important because it can form a shape like an eggshell to protect the life inside that has a destiny to be broken at a certain point. This is not abstract shape for the sake of form. Rather I use the metaphor of a glass.

DANCE EXPERIENCE

Words of Yoshioka arranged in *butoh-fu* notation by Fraleigh.

Transformation

Begin with a glass: Improvise by holding water in your body as you would in a glass. Without the glass, the water gets spilled, but it's not the purpose to keep the water in the glass either. Let someone drink the water, but be aware of the glass container. Now let this process change further and faster through the following *butoh-fu*:

Shed Your Skin
Form and life are chasing each other,
The invisible and the visible see each other.
Produce heat through friction, and
Guide your body into a state of dance.
Balance chaos with control –
Like a calm rider on a stampeding horse.

Reflections from Yoshioka

We have so many different states of energy within; they may look like contradictions or contrasts, but actually they are all organically connected. Ugliness and beauty are also the projections of our mind. We want to divide and evaluate, otherwise we feel uncomfortable, but this is not necessarily negative. The world can exist because of its diversity. Butoh (dance) for me activates divergent body energies that are usually not seen or permitted in our daily life. In other words, as our body is a receptacle of time, we can evoke its forgotten memories through dance. Butoh has the intensity to trigger that process, because it creates heat through friction and cold through stillness. The transformations and concentrations of dancing break up the eggshell of form, melt down our armor of ego, as our stiff cells and sealed memories float in the primal liquid of time.

DANCE EXPERIENCE

Connections

Use the following words of Yoshioka as mystical *butoh-fu* to inspire a dance of elemental connections and self-affirmation:

Dancing air, water, light, and ultimately Nothingness (the void),
"I" (*Jibun*) am a part of the wholeness (*Ji* = nature, *Bun* = a division).
Everything is connected. Everything is changing. Everything is in me.

Notes on Noguchi Michizo, founder of Noguchi Taiso *(Noguchi Athletic Exercise)*

Many butoh dancers incorporate Noguchi Athletic Exercise method (*Noguchi Taiso*) in their practice as an introspective approach to explore the mind–body relationship. We see this in the workshop words of Yoshioka Yumiko above and in the work of Morita Itto and Takeuchi Mika presented next. Noguchi (1996) developed his exercises in the mid-1970s, exploring the experience of gravity through movement with minimal muscle contraction. His method of concentration and mindfulness paralleled the butoh movement originating in the turmoil of the 1960s. Thus it is not surprising that early butoh dancers who were seeking to "kill the body" found an affinity to Noguchi's *Taiso* in their butoh practice. Noguchi Michizo (1914–1998) was a high school gymnastics teacher before he left to fight in World War II. On his return to the devastation of Tokyo, he appreciated the permanency of nature and gravity; these became basic concepts for the *Noguchi Taiso* method, which eventually had a great impact on stage, art, music, and other fields in Japan.

Taiso is the Japanese word for gymnastics but *Noguchi Taiso* does not resemble gymnastics as a sport with exercises. *Noguchi Taiso* is designed to release body tension in interaction with gravity. Noguchi's exercises encourage people to feel gravity and move through letting go of muscle tension (body armor). His work is a somatic practice involving concentration, mindfulness, change, and transformation – repatterning the body through movement. Letting go allows the body to dissolve – as paradoxically, the weight of the body moves. You do not move your body: Your body moves you. In the release of tension, *Noguchi Taiso* exercises are not passive, however; they encourage active empowerment of the agent through discovery and transformation. The use of *Noguchi Taiso* in butoh practice tends to liberate dancers from preconceived reaction patterns and social forms of the body, as we see in the work of Morita and Takeuchi described next.

MORITA ITTO AND TAKEUCHI MIKA: PSYCHOSOMATICS OF BUTOH

Kasai Toshiharu, who goes by the stage name of Morita Itto, is a dancer and research psychologist who has studied and performed butoh since 1988. Morita (we use his stage name) joined the Department of Clinical Psychology, Faculty of Humanities, Sapporo Gakuin University in 2004. Since 1999, he has conducted relaxation and dance therapy workshops through his study of the body–mind relationship and the development of his Butoh Dance Method. He and his dance partner and teaching associate, Takeuchi Mika, a dancer of *GooSayTen*, have performed in Canada, Germany, Japan, Jordan, Poland, Russia, Ukraine, and the United States. Takeuchi conducts dance/movement therapy based on Morita's butoh methods and her own somatic work for the day care programs of a mental health clinic in Sapporo. She has also established the *Takeuchi Mika Butoh Institute* in Sapporo.

The teaching of Morita and Takeuchi pays great attention to the least attended aspects of movement, making use of tics, tremors, jerks, facial and bodily distortions, and falling down. Involuntary movements are appreciated as ways to explore human potential – used as keys to examine the unconscious mind through reactions or movements that are suppressed under cultural social norms. In order to elicit and accept autonomous movements, Morita and Takeuchi cultivate proprioceptive sensitivity. Relaxation lies at the core of their work, allowing people to perceive their mind–body habits more clearly.

Morita's Butoh Dance Method for psychosomatic exploration was pioneered in the 1990s through the influence of two distinguished

Figure 4.4
Photo portrait of Morita Itto and Takeuchi Mika.
Photograph by Hosokawa Kyoichi

psychosomatic methods in Japan, *Noguchi Taiso* and *Takeuchi Lesson* from Takeuchi Toshiharu, a famous drama director who integrated *Noguchi Taiso* into his somatic lessons with actors and people with hearing disabilities (Kasai [Morita] 1999). Noguchi's work provides vital links for Morita. He first learned about the influence of Noguchi on butoh dancers when he participated in the workshops of Seminaru, one of the members of *Sankai Juku* butoh dance company who taught *Noguchi Taiso* whenever he had intensive butoh workshops. Morita [Kasai] eventually conceived his butoh as "body archaeology," where forgotten or socially suppressed emotions can surface (Kasai 1999).

Morita and Takeuchi's workshop words

People can enter butoh naturally through what Nouguchi called "the god of gravity." In Noguchi's way, it is not you who moves your body, but the weight of your body that moves you. All you do is start your movement and keep feeling how the weight of each part of your body determines the movements. If you try to make your body move intentionally, it ends up with over control, excessive power and muscle tension. Mika [Takeuchi] and I invented *Arm-Standing* as a preparatory exercise for *Standing-up* position. If you try to keep the standing-up position in the way of *Noguchi Taiso*, all you do is release muscle tension, and sustain the pose with the least muscle tension as possible. In this situation, your body sways or swings to some extent naturally because of the heartbeat or breathing as if your body is blown by subtle breeze. By reducing noises coming from inside and outside, you can enhance your mind–body awareness to feel both inside and outside, and you are affected by various impulses coming from your unconsciousness and outside stimuli such as sunshine, wind, fragrance of flowers, the feeling of the floor, and birds singing. You will find you are amidst butoh when your body reaches this condition.

DANCE EXPERIENCE

In the words of Itto Morita (Kasai)

Toward A Psychosomatics of Butoh: Arm-Standing Exercise (Kasai, 2001)

Standing-up with the least muscle tension is difficult for most people to realize. As a preparation, Arm Standing is much easier because the number of related bones and joints are limited: wrists, elbows and shoulders.

- Lie down on the floor on your back. If you have back problems, you may keep your knees bent. It is not necessary to stretch your knees.
- Stretch your arms wide open [with your palms facing up] along the floor.
- Rest your arms on the floor.
- Try to touch the floor with all of your nails in order to stretch your arms farther.
- Release tension from your entire body and take a rest for a while.
- Slowly, lift your forearms, keeping your elbows on the floor, until each arm forms a right angle.
- Please keep breathing normally. Try not to close your throat when you move your arms.
- Slowly lift your entire arm. Don't move in a hurry; this is a precious moment to perceive your arm weight and encounter the "god of gravity" [phrase from *Noguchi Taiso*].
- Continue lifting your arms, raising your shoulder blades off the floor.
- Stretch your arms all the way upward. Keep this position for a while.
- Release tension from your shoulders and allow your shoulder blades to rest on the floor while your arms are kept straight upward.
- Feel your shoulder blades on the floor and try to locate the point on which the weight of the arm rested. Your shoulder blades are like a foundation upon which all of the weight of your arm rests.
- Try to suspend your arms up in the air with as little muscle tension as possible. Keep your arms in this position for a while.
- When you feel tired, release tension from your shoulders and lower your elbows to the floor gradually. Feel how heavy your arms are while lowering your arms.
- Rest your elbows on the floor. Then, release tension from your elbows, allowing your forearms to lower gradually.
- Rest your arms on the floor. Feel that your body is more relaxed and tranquil.
- Repeat the exercise a few times.
- Try to hold your arms up with as little muscle tension as possible.

When you can keep your arms up with very little muscle tension, you may notice that your arms begin to move a little bit, gradually making side-to-side movements, or circular movements. And you begin to think to yourself "My arms are beginning to move a little bit, gradually making side-to-side movements, or circular movements without making them move intentionally." If your body reacts as the way that you think, it is an example of ideomotor movement.

DANCE EXPERIENCE

In the words of Kasai and Takeuchi

"We believe that small movements matter most in butoh. You can enhance your awareness level so as to feel only 1 millimeter of change of your body parts. With delicate perception, one adjusts the body in minute movements to make breathing patterns more effective and ease back pain. When you make yourself open to something coming from within or from the outside world, what you experience depends upon how well you discern differences – your sense of hair-splitting differences in your body. The word 'hair-splitting' has positive connotation in Japan, because in this attitude, you can be freely influenced by subtle change. For us butoh is not athletic, but is a way of feeling and perceiving the inner and outer world in the subtlest way: If you realize or actualize this state with your mind–body, this is butoh per se. *Hair-splitting* is not something that you intentionally try to do, but it is something actualized by keeping open space inside your body–mind that echoes subtle change toward a gentle way of being" (email communications 2004).

Hair-splitting through Takeuchi's words for Palm Blossoming
If you try to open your firmly grasped fist, it is a palm-opening exercise. The intention of this exercise is not necessarily for you to open your palm; it asks you to explore how your fist evolves and comes to "blossom" like a flower.

The first stage:
➤ Grasp your fist firmly and keep it for about 30 seconds. (Do this exercise one hand at a time.)
➤ Start releasing tension from your fist very slowly.
➤ Perceive or "hear" the noises inside your finger joints while releasing tension.
➤ Don't stop the self-opening movements of your fist.

The second stage:

➤ No muscle tension is left in your fingers that fixed your fingers.

➤ Find a way that enables your fingers to extend naturally.

➤ If your fingers move with "noises" as if driven by gears, smooth the way.

➤ Explore how your fingers and your hand are related to your arm angle, and your body form.

The first time you do this exercise, the "noises" of your fingers usually irritate you. Trying to achieve the little-noisy or noiseless movement makes this exercise a "hair-splitting" one. I like watching the setting sun, a blossoming flower for 10–20 minutes, and seem to get a hint of smooth and continuous movements.

TAKENOUCHI ATSUSHI'S *JINEN BUTOH*

Takenouchi Atsushi is a third-generation butoh dancer who appreciates the work of Hijikata, but has taken his own unique direction. He danced from age eighteen to twenty-four in *Hopo Buto Ha*, the company of Bishop Yamada, or Yamada Ippei. Hijikata choreographed *Takazashiki* (1984) for Yamada's company – Takenouchi's last performance with them. He has been working on his own *Jinen Butoh* since 1986 and created solos *Tanagokoro* (The Palm) and *Itteki* (One Drop) as universal expressions of nature, earth, and ancient times. He toured Japan between 1996 and 1999, and says he studied "the universe as spirit under Ohno Kazuo and his son Yoshito." He toured *Sun & Moon* in 1999, and led butoh workshops in Europe and Asia for six months. Since then, his tours have included natural materials musician Komiya Hiroko. Now she makes the music and sound for most of his performances. Takenouchi danced *Stone* (July 2005), a solo performance, in Avignon Festival in France, and choreographed a butoh procession through Avignon city in the festival. Now in his forties, Takenouchi has danced in several countries and in every corner of Japan, exploring the terrain of his homeland through environmental and theatrical works. He stages butoh rituals in social and natural environments.

When Takenouchi struck out to perform his own butoh style at age twenty-four, his association with nature was most important, and has remained the guiding influence of his work:

Figure 4.5
Takenouchi
Atsushi in
Turn.
Photograph by
Konronsha

I began working with children, parents, and young people, teaching them in very simple ways how to dance, cook, and make natural dyes from plants – how to make sculpture, pictures, calligraphy, and visual artifacts from natural materials. *DANCE WITH NATURE* was the name of my first school. We explored how to dance with trees, fire, water, and wind. I also used a lot of animal movement, as butoh does, but freely choreographing in my way.

(Ibid., see also Fraleigh 2005: 336)

Takenouchi's butoh respects Japanese animism, he says: "The very wide meaning of *Jinen* is that everything exists inside a living God." Ohno Kazuo and Yoshito made a deep impression on his *Jinen* thinking, Takenouchi says. He dances the experiential connections:

Sometimes I dance out my great sadness or happiness. I lost a good friend in the Kobe earthquake, so I went there to the place of destruction and danced my grief. I also dance on the killing fields of war, in Cambodia, Poland, Japan, and continuing on. I want to feel places where great masses of people have died together, to touch the natural human feeling, not in a choreographed butoh style, but directly in my dance. Like everything else, the killing fields are already dancing. So when I enter the dance already taking place, I am asking 'what is human life, what is darkness, what is death.' I touch the human crisis there. I look with touch, and touch with looking; something happens inside me when I touch death. After that I don't think anymore; I pray and I dance.

(Ibid.)

Takenouchi's workshop words on *Jinen*

In ALL things there lives God – the flow of the river of the universe that embraces the sun and moon, and the earth that is the origin of the birthing of all nature including man. God lives within man, plants, animals, and even in man-made things like houses. *Jinen* is the word that describes the universe, its origin and natural course. All things connect to this river, and are part of the river of *Jinen*.

Man generally receives beautiful forms from nature, such as the plants or animals. However, the breath of this planet also has destructive force; the swirl of the river of the universe embraces all life and death, light and dark. This is *Jinen*. There is nothing Man can do. All that I was able to do after the earthquake was to live with the people who had encountered life and death, and to pray and dance with them. The *Jinen* view of nature exists in the art forms created by ancient people. Every life form performs the dance of life and death. *Jinen Butoh* joins together with all the life that is already dancing. When we dance *Jinen*, we remove the wall of consciousness that perceives the individual " I ".

DANCE EXPERIENCE

Words of Takenouchi as translated by Nakamura

Preparation: butoh-fu on Jinen

Embracing and Becoming
Air, Sun, Huge Ancient Tree, Spacious Land
Beautiful Baby, Bird with a Broken Feather,
Blind Five-Year Old Child
Wandering Elderly Person
A person who is going to be shot
Child Dying of Starvation, Insane Soldier
Sad, Blue Moon, God of Wind and Rain in a Rage
Joyous God of Sake
A Person with Alzheimer's Disease, or Depression
Dead Bodies of the Earth, A Pile of Skull and Bones,
Your Coming Death
Memory of Sadness and Happiness
Light and Darkness, Life and Death of all the Living

Concrete method: Embrace and Transform

➤ Prepare with the *butoh-fu* above, and then let your own images emerge.

➤ Don't use technique or form. Connect with your true heart to become one with your image.

➤ From the center of your body, move your two arms as if they are a thousand arms folded into your body, begin slowly folding outward from the core of your center.

➤ From a limitless place, unfold and extend yourself as you move your arms toward an image of something you want to become.

➤ Then slowly come face to face with the image you want to become and embrace it.

➤ Bring it into your own body; your body will transform, and you will become your image. Like *Senju Kannon* the goddess with one thousand arms, who embraces the universe with her arms and transforms into the universe, you become what you embrace.

➤ Continue to repeat the cycle: *Embrace and Transform.*

Include breath and voice

➤ After that, exhale from your hara (just below the navel) saying, or voicing AOUN as in meditation.

➤ Incrementally, from closed-mouth to mouth-wide-open, begin to voice AOUN. First, with the mouth closed, produce a humming sound N , a place of nothingness.

➤ With the mouth open slightly, voice A , a place of beginning.

➤ Finally, with your mouth widely open, voice O , representing the universe.

➤ Then, beginning to close your mouth, voice U , a place of embracement, until you come back to the closed-mouth humming sound of N , a place of entering the body.

➤ Therefore you are producing NAOU, or AOUN.

➤ One cycle of voicing AUON should be done in one long, slow breath.

➤ Take a deep breath and continue to repeat the cycle.

Through practicing this cyclic process of embracing and voicing, you move without form toward various inner life transformations. Allow these transformations to move you in your dance.

FRANCES BARBE AND THE PRACTICE OF *BUTOH-FU*

Frances Barbe was born in 1971 and has been studying butoh since 1992 when she was introduced to it in Australia. Before that, she had trained in ballet and modern dance from an early age and studied theatre at university. All of her choreographic works since 1992 reflect the powerful influence of butoh. She choreographs for her own company, now based in London, and has also performed for Endo Tadashi's *Mamu Dance Theatre*, based in Germany since 1997. She has taught butoh in many contexts working with professional dancers, actors and singers, as well as in drama and dance schools. She has received several research grants to pursue historical and theoretical studies of butoh and Japanese culture, including the prestigious Daiwa/AHRB Creative Fellowship in

Figure 4.6
Frances Barbe's work
Palpitation (2003).
Photograph by
Reuben Hart

2001. Having co-founded *Theatre Training Initiative* in 2000, an organisation providing professional development training for performers, Barbe also directed the *Daiwa International Butoh Festival* in London in 2005.

Barbe's workshop words on *butoh-fu*

Intrigued by the ideas of *butoh-fu* described in Waguri Yukio's (1998) CD-Rom and in Kurihara Nanako's article, 'The Words of Butoh' (2000), I decided to explore *butoh-fu* for myself in practice. For a long time I deliberately avoided using Hijikata Tatsumi's own words, thinking it was better to find my own words and images, soon I realized that understanding Hijikata's way with words was a crucial step in innovating the way I used words myself. There was something different going on in butoh's use of words than in other forms of dance I had experienced, where of course, words and images were also used. Was it the kinds of words and images used that differed? Was there a difference of purpose in the dance forms?

I started playing with Hijikata's *butoh-fu* 'You Live Because Insects Eat You' as documented by Waguri Yukio on his CD-Rom – *Butoh-Kaden*. The exercise below is the result of this play that I am refining and developing all the time. It does not profess to be "the way" of working with *butoh-fu*, but is just the way I have tried so far. If it is a misunderstanding of *butoh-fu*, at least it has been a very fruitful one for me.

Butoh-fu: You Live Because Insects Eat You
Hijikata Tatsumi's words, recorded by Waguri Yukio

A person is buried in a wall.
S/he becomes an insect.
The internal organs are parched and dry.
The insect is dancing on a thin sheet of paper.
The insect tries to hold falling particles from its own body,
And dances, making rustling noises.
The insect becomes a person, who is wandering around,
So fragile, s/he could crumble at the slightest touch.

Preparatory instructions for practice
These are things to think about for the DANCE EXPERIENCE that follows. When the lines of the text are spoken, respond to the image with your

body. Don't think about a literal miming of the words. Allow the images to act on and change your body. What are the implications of these images for your senses? What do they suggest to the stance or the form of the body? The verbs are often keys that suggest movement, rhythm and quality or texture. Work intuitively. There is no one right way to respond – so don't analyze, respond.

When I am teaching, I ask students to stay with one image as long as I repeat it or until I speak the next one. I tell them: "When you do move on, don't skip over the process of change; this is one of the main points of this exercise. Take your time, and really explore how the body transforms from one thing to another, and how there is a moment when you are *between two states*.

DANCE EXPERIENCE

By Frances Barbe

These are the key things I emphasize in the practice of *butoh-fu*:

➤ Keep a deep concentration and focus at all times. It doesn't work if you look around the room with the same eyes you use in everyday life.

➤ If you don't hear a particular word, don't break out and look at the teacher, or ask. When I teach, I repeat the images several times, because the concentration engages the dancer's body at the deepest level of creativity. It is also important for creating a particular energy in the space, so that it seems the space is changing at the same time as the dancing body.

First phase

➤ Stand in a very prepared, ready state, facing any direction you like. Take a simple, neutral form or stance.

➤ We want to see how the first image enters your body and changes it, so it is important to start with a clear, empty body.

➤ The workshop leader speaks the lines, repeating the image, and leaving space to watch the dancers' responses.

> A person is buried in a wall.
> S/he becomes an insect.
> The internal organs are parched and dry.
> The insect is dancing on a thin sheet of paper.

The insect tries to hold falling particles from its own body,
And dances, making rustling noises.
The insect becomes a person, who is wandering around,
So fragile, s/he could crumble at the slightest touch.

➤ Come to stillness. ... And finish.

Second phase

Now we repeat the exercise in two groups so participants have the chance to work with the images more than once, and so they can watch each other. It is not necessary to repeat exactly the same forms, new ones can be found each time, but it can be useful to repeat a form that has potential, so that it can be experienced more deeply.

Third phase

Next you can go through the transformations without me talking, because you know the sequence. Listen to the energy of the room so that you can experience the difference and similarities between the bodies in the space. (This can be done in silence or with music.)

Fourth phase

Repeat the whole process using your own *butoh-fu*. Below is an example of one I have written:

Butoh-fu: Woman in the Swamp
By Frances Barbe, Nov 2004

At the bottom of a swamp sits a woman.
A sound awakens her body to motion.
She emerges dripping to the surface, with creatures and moss
    sticking to her.
She walks across Monet's Water Lilies, smelling with her ears and
    arms for the sound that awoke her.
Her tail darts behind her, guiding her direction.
Her flashing eyes of fire throw dangerous glances into space.
Attacked by darts from within her body, her torso is pierced.
She is emptied through these holes.
Air rushes into the empty body and she becomes a spirit.
Melting back into the water, she floats on its current.

Writing, speaking, and dancing your own butoh-fu

➤ Write your *butoh-fu* quickly, intuitively, without thinking too much. Remember it is not a linear story that has to make sense but a poem of transformations that intends to provoke dance from the body.

➤ In pairs, speak your *butoh-fu* for your partner to respond to, as you practiced with the workshop leader. Perhaps your partner can show you possibilities that would not have occurred to you? Change over, so that you both get to speak and dance your *butoh-fu*.

➤ Discuss what you saw in your partner's response to your images. What did you like? What was surprising? What did not engage you at all?

➤ If you perform for an audience, keep in mind the point is not to mime or illustrate the images, but to affect a transformation of the body, which provokes the audience to imagine and project their own stories onto the bodies.

➤ Give feedback to the creator of the *butoh-fu*. Were the images they gave full of potential? Rich in sensual information? Were they too intellectual to really enliven the body?

You can repeat this process several times, even combining several *butoh-fu* into a journey of change. Ultimately you might end up with a small choreography that has deep and rich images at its heart.

Note for choreographers and directors

This can be a useful process for choreographers and directors to go through, as it develops your ability to give a very specific image for performers to embody without dictating the solution to them, thereby opening a work to greater possibilities.

HARADA NOBUO: BUTOH IS EVERYTHING

Harada Nobuo practiced butoh with Kasai Akira's *Tenshi-kan* (House of Angels) from 1973–1979. When Kasai disbanded *Tenshi-kan* to go to Europe to study, Harada founded *Seiryukai* (Blue Dragon Group) at the same location. He taught and performed there from 1980–1985 when he left Tokyo to return to his ancestral home in Yanagawa, Kyushu. After a nine-year hiatus from butoh, Harada founded *Seiryukai* in Fukuoka in 1994. The group is active in practice and performances with groups with physical and psychological challenges and the community at large.

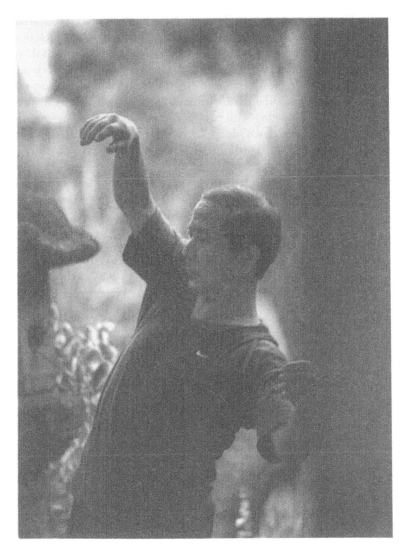

Figure 4.7 Harada Nobuo improvises at Shimada Art Museum. Photograph by Imamura Kaoru

For Harada, everything we do everyday is butoh. Harada is inspired by and inspires by moving with his students. It is difficult to pick out particular stages from his butoh workshop since the whole workshop seems to develop seamlessly. The workshop is not shaped by instruction. Nobody develops the workshop, and everybody develops the workshop. It is a communal act and it is a community act. To move in any way you wish to move, interacting with people as you move past them or with them at a very slowed down pace, allows you to experience yourself and them in a naked way – no instructions about what to do, how to move, what to feel, what to think, how to act. This allows the mover, or forces the mover, to let the expectations of what they are supposed to do peel away. Each mover may have a very different meaning and experience. Tamah Nakamura explains a typical workshop:

Everyone gathers in the practice room in the evening about 7 o'clock. After warming up, the group begins moving slowly, feet barely lifting from the polished floor, sliding as if across ice or a plate of glass a centimeter at a time. Eyes gaze unfocused. As the workshop progresses into free movement, over the next hour and a half, participants flow in and out of individual movement, small group, and large group interaction, to movement suggestions offered by Harada.

Harada's workshop words on Becoming a Wave

Recorded and translated by Tamah Nakamura

Become a Wave
Daily we breathe in and breathe out without conscious awareness. Let's try to control this process consciously.

First phase
➤   First, breathe in deeply, and then slowly breathe out completely emptying your belly of air.
➤   As you breathe out, move your tailbone toward the floor as you gently and calmly move into a crouch sitting on your heels. Imagine your tailbone rooting deeply into the earth.
➤   Imagine a rod running through your center from head to foot. From the crouching position, very slowly begin rising to a standing position feeling the rod grounding you and pulling you down.

Second phase

➤ In the full standing position, imagine a translucent thread rising from the top of your head drawing you up toward the sky. Holding the feeling of being pulled up, slowly begin descending into a crouch on your heels.

➤ Repeat: rising and descending with these images as slowly as you can.

Third phase

➤ From a full standing position, imagine someone pulling you from behind. Incline your body forward. Then incline your body in all directions as you sense a pull in the opposite direction.

➤ Continue sensing an opposing pull as you lift your arm, lift your leg, turn in a circle, run, jump, fall down. No matter how violent your movements are, observe them calmly.

➤ See yourself. Then see another self.

In the center of that observation process exists the center of spiritual balance. From this spiritual center, interact joyfully with countless rippling threads of light radiating outward. You have become a wave rolling in and out. You are lightness and darkness. You have become yourself.

DANCE EXPERIENCE

Tree: connecting with our inner selves

We begin by standing up and holding the lost feeling of not knowing how to move. Seiryukai's improvisational exercises in dance class typically begin with painstakingly slow, careful steps as if petrified in a tight corner. We imagine carrying a delicate, precious object across the room to give to an imaginary person. We slowly cross the stage, a mountain, a river, the sea, calmly, alone, and together. We then discover a way to move alone and together. Momentary discoveries of reality occur through a connection of the inner force with bodily form. (Nakamura, Seiryukai workshop, November 2001).

First phase: individual exploration

➤ You are a tree. Stay perfectly still. You are a tree. A tree does not move.

➤ Feel the roots of your tree go deep down from your feet into the floor and into the ground beneath the floor. A tree only moves when the environment influences it.

➤ Where will that movement energy come from? Sense the environment.

➤ The wind gently blows and rustles your leaves. The sun pours down on you and warms you. Your leaves are stirred by the wind and turn toward the warm sun.

➤ You are rooted deeply sensing the elements in the environment around you.

Second phase: group exploration

➤ Start with two people standing on each side of the room, then move in minute increments toward the tree sensing everyone's energy and focusing it toward the center – toward the tree.

➤ As you reach her, move near her and surround her, standing and squatting, sending in your energy and gathering back the energy. Do this for about 5 minutes.

➤ Stop, be still and hold your position for a while longer gathering in everyone's energy.

➤ See yourself, see another self, and see yourself in the other.

Third phase: grounding and centering

➤ Stand in a circle and use your hands to sweep off all the excess scattered energy from all (tree) limbs of your body, from head down to arms down to legs and feet.

➤ Use a lightly closed fist to pat the body all over in the same routine, closing the pores.

➤ Now sit together in a circle *seiza* style (sit with legs folded under body), intertwining hands with fingers, and on the count of three bring your cupped hands to your belly chakra with an expulsion of voiced breath, "EI", centering your energy.

➤ This grounds you and returns you to your physical body.

➤ Gather your belongings and walk back out into the world in a form the society recognizes and accepts but with a new experience of knowing who you are.

Nakamura's reflections

These explorations, which describe workshop segments of a full day of activities, are part of my Ph.D. study, "Beyond Performance in Japanese Butoh Dance: Embodying Re-Creation of Self and Social Identities," Fielding Graduate University, 2006. In my dissertation, I examine relational connections of *Butoh Seiryukai* participants to others in the group and to the larger society. The results show that *Seiryukai*, through its non-performance orientation, provides an important social space for interaction, *Ba* in Japanese. The inclusive group structure encourages self-development of participants through somatic and verbal dialogue.

WAGURI YUKIO AND *BUTOH-KADEN* CD-ROM

Waguri Yukio was a disciple of Hijikata from 1972 until Hijikata's death in 1986 except for a leave from 1970–1984 when he was a Kimono dyer. He currently tours domestically and internationally presenting butoh workshops, lectures and performances either solo or with his group *Butoh Kohzensha*. *Kohzensha* is the name given to him by his master, Hijikata.

From 1972–1978 he was the main male dancer at Hijikata's *Asbestos-kan* and during that time he carefully recorded Hijikata's *butoh-fu* words and images for choreography. After a quarter of a century, in 1998, Waguri has made Hijikata's *butoh-fu* available in his CD-Rom titled *Butoh-Kaden* (1998). Even Hijikata did not publicize his own *butoh-fu* method until just before his death, and then it was in an informal manner. The strong impetus for Waguri to organize and publish his teacher's choreography occurred in 1988–1989 when he joined Nakajima Natsu on her tour of Europe: *Nemuri to Tensei* (Sleep and Reincarnation: From Empty Land). The challenge to properly teach the method to dancers of all different nationalities proved "painful" and was the catalyst for the creation of activities leading to the production of the *Butoh-Kaden* CD-Rom. In 1992 he started the Hijikata Study Method Group, and in 1996 performed "*Butoh-Kaden*", a journey of seven *butoh-fu* worlds. This performance serves as the basis for the *butoh-fu* structure that is revealed in Disk A.

Waguri's exposition of Hijikata's *butoh-fu* is the first and, to date, only published source through which the public can access the process of Hijikata's *butoh-fu*. The two disks in the package provide explanations, analysis and photographs of the structural aspect of Hijikata's butoh method. A hardcover manual guides the viewer with instructions in Japanese and English. Most material on Hijikata and his *butoh-fu* is archived at the Keio University Research Center for the Arts and Arts Administration in Tokyo, requiring a physical visit to access the archives. *Butoh-Kaden* offers students, researchers and people with an interest in Hijikata's method a rich diversified view of aspects of butoh easily accessible in one collection.

Disk A contains a database of eighty-eight of Hijikata's *butoh-fu* recorded by Waguri in his notes, and segments of Waguri's *Butoh-Kaden* performance. The *butoh-fu* (butoh notes) in this disk reveal structured choreography created by Hijikata for Waguri's dances. These serve as examples of Hijikata's structured method since other disciples will have different *butoh-fu* in their notes for their own dances. Waguri systematizes his notes into a map of seven integrated worlds. His analysis of the *butoh-fu* is based on systematization into these seven worlds. The *butoh-fu* may sound poetic, but each word refers to a dance form and a movement of the body in space.

Disk B provides information on butoh in general, fifty essays on butoh, and butoh dancers with their photos from four separate schools: Hijikata Tatsumi, Ohno Kazuo, Kasai Akira, and Maro Akaji. A chronology of Hijikata's works from the late 1950s to 1986 includes photos, film, and voice. The film is a clip from *Nikutai no haran* (Rebellion of the Body, 1968), which was introduced in Chapter 3. The Hijikata vocal with an English script option is from *A Bird with Mercy Comes with the Fluttering of Wing Skeleton*, the introduction to Chapter 2 as words of Hijikata. This is from his spoken monologue of 1976, also translated more closely as he created his title: *The CoMPaSSioNaTe SouL BiRD comes to unfurl its rustling SKeleTaL WiNGS*.

We see in *Soul Bird*, the inimitable style that founded butoh – as Japanese writer Nario Goda puts it – "Hijikata threw the first stone."

ENGLISH GLOSSARY OF TERMS

English terms include Japanese words that are in common use in English. Japanese words are italicized, except for the word "butoh" (when used by itself), now understood internationally as a form of dance originating in Japan. Special attention is given to words that have sprung up in the practice of butoh. Some of the Japanese words also appear in the Japanese Glossary of Terms with Japanese ideograms and are indicated here with an asterisk*.

aesthetics 11

   1) From the Greek *Aisthesis* meaning perception. 2) A branch of philosophy that studies art, originally the study of the beautiful, but now including concerns for subject/object relationships, expression, perception and insight.

Albee, Edward, born 1928 78

   An American playwright producing plays in the same surrealist vein that inspired Hijikata.

alchemy 13

   1) An early form of chemistry seeking to transform base metals into gold and to discover a universal cure of disease. 2) Pertaining to magical powers of enchantment or transformation.

Amagatsu, Ushio, born 1949 11

Founder and choreographer of the butoh company, *Sankai Juku*, grounded spiritually in the pre-history of the body. Powdered rice white dancers of this all male company are famous early in their development for their upside down hanging dances, later for architectural, highly polished and mystical butoh. *Sankai Juku* performs in major venues worldwide.

Ando, Mitsuko 8

A disciple of Eguchi, and one of Hijikata's modern dance teachers.

Ankoku Butoh* 1

Butoh means "dance step," and *Ankoku* is "darkness." Hijikata named his dance "Ankoku Butoh," dance of darkness.

archetype 1

1) A model or life pattern. 2) In psychology a memory, image, or symbol in dream or myth.

Argentina, La (1888–1936) 25

With the professional name of Antonia Mercé, an Argentine-born Spanish dancer, who was a great influence on Spanish dance and the butoh of Ohno Kazuo.

Artaud, Antonin (1896–1948) 84

French poet, dramatist, and actor, who influenced the development of experimental theater – especially the theater of the absurd, environmental, and ritual theater. He used the term "theater of cruelty" to define a new theater that forced audiences to confront the primal self, stripped of social conventions. He minimized spoken word and sets, relying on a combination of physical movement, gesture, and sounds. His book *The Theatre and Its Double* (1938; translated to English 1958) describes theatrical modes that became traits of experimental theater.

Asbestos-kan* (*Asbestos Studio*) 22

Asbestos school and butoh company founded by Hijikata Tatsumi and his wife Motofuji Akiko. Motofuji's father had been an Asbestos salesman. The school is sometimes spelled *Asbesutosukan*.

Ashikawa, Yoko 3

Protégé of Hijikata, the woman who embodied Hijikata's

choreography and concepts so fully in performance that she effected a shift from male to female sensibility in butoh.

avant-garde 8

In art and theater: new, experimental, or unconventional.

Ballets Russes 16

Russian émigré ballet company that toured outside Russia from 1909 to 1929 under the direction of Russian impresario Sergey Diaghilev and featured such stars as Vaslav Nijinsky (1890–1950).

Barbe, Frances, born 1971 102

British butoh dancer, who also trained in ballet and modern dance and has studied Suzuki theater methods. All of her choreographic works since 1992 reflect the powerful influence of butoh. She choreographs for her own company, now based in London, and has also performed for Endo Tadashi's *Mamu Dance Theatre*.

Bausch, Pina, born 1940 16

German dancer. Choreographer and director of *Tanztheater Wuppertal* known internationally for her revival of expressionist dance and her bold total theater works.

Beckett, Samuel (1906–1989) 78

Irish born poet, novelist, and playwright. Author of the surrealist play *Waiting for Godot*, one of Hijikata's inspirations.

bestiality 78

Human sexual acts with animals.

Brecht, Bertolt (1898–1956) 48

One of the most influential German dramatists and theoreticians of the theater in the twentieth century, beginning his career at the height of German Expressionism.

Buddhism 48

A world religion and philosophy based on the teachings of the Buddha, based in the belief that the Buddha mind pervades everything and everyone, grounded in the practice of meditation for psychophysical benefits and enlightenment.

Butoh* 1

A form of dance originating in Japan in the turbulence of the 1960s, principally through the dance works and teachings of Hijikata Tatsumi. *Butoh* in Japanese means simply – dance step.

Butoh-fu* 3
Poetic word and visual imagery used to inspire butoh choreography and performance. *Fu* means chronicle. *Butoh-fu* are also considered a form of dance notation, a score for performance, or a record.

Butohist* 17
Those who maintain and perform the spirit of butoh. Hijikata and Ohno provide the word its original meaning.

Cunningham, Merce, born 1919 16
American modern dancer and choreographer, a leader of the avant-garde in American dance, and harbinger to the postmodern dance.

dadaism 49
This aesthetic movement, also called Da Da, is a European artistic and literary movement of the early twentieth century characterized by absurdity, anarchy, irrationality, and irreverence.

Dance Macabre 41
Dance of Death – originally from medieval times – also referring to the epidemic of the black plague.

Daruma* 5
In Japan, a *Daruma* is a limbless figure (or doll) weighted so that it bounces back when knocked over. It is a symbol of persistence leading to success. *Daruma* is also an abbreviation for *Bodhidharma*, a mythical Middle Eastern priest said to have carried Zen practice and teachings to China about 500 BC.

deconstruction 73
1) A literary movement that began with continental philosophers, such as Jacques Derrida, who began to question the prominent place of the author in writing. 2) A method of analyzing texts (including dance as a form or text) based on the belief that language is unstable and that the reader is central in constructing meaning. 3) To take something apart.

Delsarte, François (1811–1871) 16
French singer, philosopher, and teacher, whose philosophy of dance gestures and expressions of the human body was highly influential in the development of modern dance.

Denishawn 16

A school of dancing founded by early modern dancers Ruth St. Denis and Ted Shawn. Denis drew inspiration from the Orient. Shawn sought an authentic inclusion of masculine power in dance.

eclecticism 16

In art and dance: a mixture of aesthetic sources and styles, sometimes a mixture of diverse cultural elements.

Edo * 11

The original name for Tokyo. The *Edo* period in Japanese history is from 1603 to 1868.

Eguchi, Takaya 9

A dancer who studied with Mary Wigman early in the twentieth century and imported the creative experiments and developmental physical techniques of German *Neue Tanz* to Japan. Eguchi's teaching spread two ways in Japan: toward the growth of lyric and dramatic modern dance through such contemporary artists as Kanai Fumie (who became his assistant), and also toward the more gestural and raw dance of butoh through Ohno and Hijikata, even as their butoh represented a break with modern dance.

empathy/empathetic 3

To be moved by someone or something. To appreciate a feeling held in common with another person or others in a group.

ethnography/ethnographic 2

A research method that requires the researcher to be both a participant and an observer in a setting to understand the meaning of interaction in a specific culture, such as a butoh group, for example. Interviews and artifacts often provide sources of understanding.

ethos 69

A matrix (often cultural or ethical) of values, attitudes, habits, or beliefs.

existentialism 74

A philosophical and literary movement emphasizing individual existence, freedom, and choice that influenced many writers in the 19th and 20th centuries. Existentialism holds that individuals are responsible for their own actions and rejects the idea of predestination.

expressionism 2

An imprecise term, referring to art and literature that attempts to convey a subjective, psychological, or spiritual essence. See also German expressionism.

Genet, Jean (1910–1986) 8

French novelist and dramatist, whose writings reveal bizarre and sometimes grotesque aspects of human existence, expressing undercurrents of life and death. Genet is the literary inspiration behind Hijikata's performative surrealism; he choreographed *Diviinu sho* (Divine) for Ohno, a solo based on *Divine* the hero/ine of Genet's novel *Our Lady of the Flowers*.

German expressionism 14

An artistic movement that originated in Germany between 1905 and 1925 whose advocates sought to represent feelings and moods rather than objective reality, using bold colors and forms in highly stylized and subjective manners of representation. In dance, Rudolph von Laban and Mary Wigman present the primary examples. Laban later became famous as a movement theorist and not as an expressionist artist. Wigman, while also advocating "pure dance," remains the root of expressionist dance forms. Modern/ postmodern dancers such as Susanne Linke still hark back to her work. Eguchi Takaya, the teacher of Ohno Kazuo, studied with Wigman. Ohno was also influenced by another famous German expressionist, and student of Wigman's – Harald Kreutzberg.

grotesque 21

1) Ugly, misshapen, and distorted. 2) Repugnant.

Haiku 40

A traditional and spare form of Japanese poetry often composed in three lines of 5/7/5 that equal seventeen syllables. Some poems are slightly longer or shorter. *Haiku* is a folk-art and not the special province of professional poets. There have been famous *Haiku* poets – like Basho – and there is a particular kind of Zen *Haiku* as well, indicating the season of the year within the poetic image.

Harada, Nobuo, born 1949 39

Practiced butoh with Kasai Akira's *Tenshi-kan* (House of Angels) from 1973–1979 and founded *Seiryukai* (Blue Dragon Group) at the same location in Tokyo. Harada taught and performed there from 1980–1985; he founded *Seiryukai* in Fukuoka in 1994. The group is active in performances with groups with physical and psychological challenges and the community at large. For Harada, "everything we do is butoh."

Hijikata, Tatsumi (1928–1986) 1
Principle founder and source of butoh. His specific designation of his form of dance is *Ankoku Butoh* (Darkness Dance).

Hokohtai * 107
Also *Hoko*, "The walking body" in butoh, with a lowered center and slightly bent knees, eternally slow and stylized in various ways, sometimes shedding style, engendering a low threshold of presence, a "dropping away" of body consciousness as the dancer enters a meditative state of slow motion.

Hosoe, Eikoh, born 1933 13
Born Hosoe Toshiro in Yonezawa, Yamagata prefecture. Hosoe is an integral part of the history of butoh, as a friend of Hijikata, and the photographer who caught something of the essence of Hijikata's butoh, especially in his striking photographs of Hijikata in the Tohoku landscape in his book *Kamaitachi* (Sickle-Weasel, 1969). Hosoe is also working on a book of photographs of Ohno Kazuo.

impressionism 2
A style of painting and music, especially of late nineteenth and early twentieth century France, characterized by the use of rich harmonies and tones to express scenes or emotions. Impressionists such as Vincent Van Gogh and Degas were strongly influenced by the abstract, suave and flowing style of the Japanese *Ukiyo-e* artists.

improvisation/improvisational 3
In dance: 1) Performing impromptu. 2) Performing without set choreography. 3) Improvisation in dance may involve some structure, but not set and textually specific movements.

Japan–US Security Treaty 73
Beginning with Japan's surrender on September 2, 1945, the Allies placed the country under the control of a U.S. army. Finally, to ensure Japan's defense and secure it as an ally of the United States, the two countries signed a bilateral mutual security treaty.

Jinen* 1
The universe, the river of its origin and natural course.

Joyce, James (1882–1941) 43
Irish author and one of the foremost literary figures of the twentieth century, whose writings feature revolutionary innovations. Joyce is best known for his epic novel *Ulysses* (1922), which uses a literary technique called "stream of consciousness" that attempts to portray the flow of thoughts in a person's mind.

Jung, Carl Gustav (1875–1961) 43
Swiss psychiatrist and one of the founding fathers of modern depth psychology. His most influential concept, the collective unconscious profoundly affected psychology, philosophy, and the arts. Jung broke with Sigmund Freud in the early history of psychoanalytic thought, inspiring interest in Eastern religions, the *I Ching*, and the power of myth. He taught that the artist is a vehicle for the unconscious psychic life of mankind.

Kabuki Theater 11
Created by Izumono Okuni *c.* 1600; its roots lie in Bunraku Puppet Theater and Noh Theater. Initially played by all women which was banned by the government and today's actors are all men. It is one of the three major traditional theater arts in Japan along with Noh and Kyogen.

Kamaitachi* (Sickle-Weasel, 1969) 32
Hosoe Eikoh's book of photographs of Hijikata, immortalizing butoh in compelling outdoor portraits of the dancer in the rustic fields of Tohoku.

Kamihitoe* 115
Hair-split difference.

Kasai, Akira, born 1943 13
Contemporary butohist who departed from the work of Hijikata, but nevertheless takes inspiration from Hijikata and Ohno, also using eurythmy, a dance like form of body training founded by the mystic philosopher Rudolph Steiner in 1921 that he studied in Germany in 1979. Founder of *Tenshikan* dance company (House of the Angels) early in his career, now an independent artist performing and teaching internationally.

Koan* 48

A *koan* is a riddle-like question (or paradox) in the practice of some forms of Zen Buddhism – used to baffle the rational mind, and as a tool in meditation to quell the forward momentum or business of the mind. "What was my face before my parents were born?" is a *koan*, as well as "What is *Mu* (Emptiness)"? A *koan* is not meaningless, and teachers of Zen often expect true answers or responses to the questions. There are no fixed answers, however, they vary according to circumstances and the quest. The answers ride on the practice of meditation and intuition, and cannot be reasoned or willed.

Konpaku* 59

World of the dead explained in Buddhist thought – a place that cannot be seen where the dead come and go several times a year crossing the river to their ancestral homes. It describes the riverbanks where the dead and the living travel very much at peace with themselves.

Ledoh 17

Dancer from Burma with his butoh company *Salt Farm* based in San Francisco, California.

Meiji restoration (1868) 18

A political revolution in Japan that overthrew the Tokugawa shogunate (military government) in January 1868 and replaced it with the emperor *Meiji* who was emperor from 1867 to 1912. This restoration (revolution) marks a tide of modernization and youthful reformers.

metamorphosis 2

Change of physical form, a transformation.

Mishima, Yukio (1925–1970) 8

Pseudonym of Hiraoka Kimitake, Japanese novelist who writes about the dichotomy between traditional Japanese values and the contemporary world. His book *Kinjiki* (Forbidden Colors) was the subject source of Hijikata's first butoh work by the same title in 1959.

MoBu 11

An aesthetic blend of modern dance and butoh.

modern dance 2

A genre of participatory and theater dance that developed throughout the twentieth century, first as a reaction against the conventions of ballet, and later as a wide collection of techniques and theater works through individual innovators such as Mary Wigman in Germany and Martha Graham and Jose Limon in America. Postmodern dance is thought to succeed the term modern dance in some accounts. Others see continuity between modern/postmodern forms.

Monet, Claude Oscar (1840–1926) 9

French painter, a leading exponent of impressionism, the late nineteenth century art movement. Monet's paintings captured scenes of everyday life and the qualities of light in nature. His use of bright colors in short strokes became an identifying mark of impressionism. As with several French impressionist painters, Monet was influenced by the style of Japanese Ukiyo-e. His idea for painting varied images of his pond garden at Giverny in several time frames came through Hokusai's *Hundred Views of Mount Fuji* and Hiroshige's *Hundred Views of Edo*.

Morita, Itto, born 1951 13

Itto was initiated into butoh by Semimaru (Sankai Juku) in 1988. After butoh activities with a troupe Kobuzoku Arutai, he started butoh duo GooSayTen with Takeuchi Mika in Sapporo in 1996, and has been exploring butoh for body–mind and spiritual integration. Professor of Department of Clinical Psychology, Sapporo Gakuin University. Board member of Japanese Dance Therapy Association.

morphology 11

The study of organic structure of bodies or words and patterns in language.

Motofuji, Akiko (1928–2003) 13

Wife of Hijikata Tatsumi, she established Asbestos Studio in 1950 where she worked as Hijikata's manager and producer. She studied modern dance and ballet from a child and was a principal dancer for Tsuda Nobutoshi.

Nakajima, Natsu 50

One of the female founders of butoh through her work with Hijikata and Ohno Kazuo and her internationally performed original choreography.

Neue Tanz 2

New Dance: modern dance as it arose in Germany through the early twentieth century with Rudolph von Laban, Mary Wigman, and such artists and Kurt Joss, and Harald Kreutzberg. See also Modern Dance and German Expressionism.

Nietzsche, Friedrich Wilhelm (1844–1900) 87

Nineteenth century German philosopher and poet who predicted the crumbling of values in the twentieth century, and whose views were influential in the dance world, particularly through the works of modernists Isadora Duncan, Martha Graham, and Doris Humphrey, as well as many postmodern artists. Nietzsche's book, *Zarathustra*, is read widely as a text dedicated to an affirmation of life through dancing and its revaluing of Christian values. "I would not believe in a God who could not dance," says Nietzsche. His philosophy is often considered as the root of existentialism and deconstruction.

Nikutai no hanran * 8

Hijikata's dance: *Rebellion of the Body* (1968).

Niwa *(1982) 110

Nakajima Natsu's full-length work *The Garden* premiered in Tokyo in 1982, one of the first butoh dances to be performed internationally by a woman, beginning with the *Festival of New Dance* in Montreal Canada in 1985. This dance develops the garden or field of a woman's life demonstrating the power and morphology of butoh.

Noguchi, Michizo (1914–1998) 13

Founder of *Noguchi Taiso* (Noguchi Athletic Exercise), used as technical practice by many butoh dancers as an introspective approach to explore the mind–body relationship. Noguchi developed his exercises in the mid-1970s, exploring the experience of gravity through movement with minimal muscle contraction. His method of concentration and mindfulness paralleled the butoh movement originating in the sociopolitical turmoil of the 1960s.

Noguchi Taiso * 120

Noguchi Athletic Exercise. See Noguchi, M. above.

Noh Theater 11

A form of classical Japanese musical drama, which grew out of various popular forms and was brought to its present aristocratic form by Zeami who taught it at court in the fifteenth century. It is one of the three officially recognized national forms of drama that include Kyogen and Kabuki.

obsessional art 74

An aesthetic expression in 1960s Japan, which rebelled against the modernism sweeping over Japan. Through obsession with images of physical deformity, violence against the body, identity and spirit obsessional art was used as a tool of rebellion for both artistic objects and the psychological state of the creative process. These Happenings and Actions as they were called can be found in the work of Hijikata Tatsumi, Mishima Yukio, Hosoe Eikoh and other avant-garde artists. The relationship between artist and action as a central concept may have expressed a criticism of Western modernist art.

Ohno, Kazuo, born 1906 1

A modern dancer who founded butoh with Hijikata Tatsumi in the 1960s. He achieved fame in Japan and internationally for such performances as *Admiring La Argentina*, *My Mother*, *The Dead Sea*, and *Water Lilies*. He introduced butoh to international audiences.

Ohno, Yoshito, born 1938 8

The son of Ohno Kazuo and his dance partner for over forty years, their joint performances include *The Old Man and the Sea* (1959), and *Water Lilies* (1987), among others. Yoshito's butoh dance experience began with Hijikata in *Kinjiki* (1959).

onomatopoeia 43

1) Words that sound like the thing or action in question, for example Splash! Hiss! and Buzz! Here is a short *Haiku* poem from the Japanese master Basho that ends in onomatopoeia: The old pond / A frog jumps in / Plop! 2) Onomatopoeia also refers to formations of words that leave a visceral trace – as in Hijikata's use of language, and that of some poets (like the surrealists).

ontic 11

An adjective, pertaining to existence or being.

ontology 54

The study of being, a general branch of metaphysics concerned with the nature of being, or a particular theory of being.

phenomenology 43

A branch of modern philosophy founded by Edmund Husserl that explains the object–subject relationship of the world of appearances – seeking to explain "things-in-themselves" and the body–mind as non-dualistic. Some of the most prominent western phenomenologists are Martin Heidegger, Merleau-Ponty, Jean Paul Sartre, and Simone de Beauvoir – in Japan – Ichikawa Hiroshi and Yuasa Yasuo.

postmodern dance 3

1) In the West, the dance that emerged first in America in the rebellious 1960s. 2) Dance forms that developed after mainstream modern dance in an objective turn away from emotion. 3) Rejection of the stylizations of modern dance as these came to prominence in the work of Martha Graham, Jose Limon, and others. 4) Dance featuring eclecticism (mixing periods and aesthetic styles). 5) In Japan, butoh is sometimes called "postmodern" because of its place in history and its eclectic mining of global sources for themes, costumes, and music.

psychosomatic 124

1) Involving both the psychological and somatic dimensions of being. 2) Sometimes used to describe a physical illness thought to have its origins in mental factors such as stress or trauma.

Rimbaud, (Jean Nicolas) Arthur (1854–1891) 22

French poet of the symbolist school who exhibited great intellectual talent and wrote verse at the age of ten. When he was 17, he composed the strikingly original poem, "The Drunken Boat." This work set the tone of the entire symbolist (also called "decadent") movement.

Sankai Juku 11

Butoh dance company founded by Amagatsu Ushio. See Amagatsu.

satyr 31

1) In Greek mythology, a creature with the body of a man and the ears, horns, and legs of a goat. 2) A man who displays unwarranted or excessive sexual behavior.

shapeshifter 5

Sometimes used as another word for "Shaman."

Shin* 114

Center/Heart/Core/Tree Trunk/Spirit/Body.

somatics 101

A field of study that develops somatic practices of embodiment through movement therapy and movement re-education, also referring to a field of psychology that gives primary attention to embodiment and perception. From the Greek *Soma*: 1) the body as perceived by the self, a first person understanding of self, and the body as experienced. 2) In the nervous system, each neuron is composed of a cell body called a soma, a major fiber called an axon, and a system of branches called dendrites.

Su-En, aka Susanna Akerlund 17

Butoh dancer and choreographer from Sweden who was given her butoh name by her teacher Ashikawa Yoko.

surrealism 2

1) A complex early twentieth century movement in art and literature creating fantastic, erotic imagery in juxtapositions of dream states and reality that seem to contradict each other. 2) An avant-garde movement rejecting existing aesthetic cannons and based on radical experimentation. 3) As a performative rather than product-oriented movement, surrealism carries through a political purpose of questioning social mores. 4) Now more commonly understood as inspiring artistic strategies of resistance to established rules and norms – also drawing from dream states and subconscious life through active imagination. 5) In automatist prose and poetry the surrealists allowed their thoughts to flow freely without attempting to edit them. 6) The surrealist writers revived interest in two nineteenth century French poets whose works anticipate the surrealists: Arthur Rimbaud and Isidore Ducasse with the pen name, Le Comte de Lautréamont. Hijikata's writings and dances include references to the surrealist movement, and also to Rimbaud.

symbol 5

A symbol stands for or represents something else, and often depends on context.

symbolism 2

1) A nineteenth century literary and artistic movement that sought

to evoke ideas of feelings through the use of symbolic images. 2) Art that reveals ideas or truths through the use of abstract symbols. 3) The use of symbols to invest things with a representative meaning. 4) In psychologically oriented art and mythology, a symbol is some-times used to represent an impulse or wish that has been repressed or hidden. In Jungian psychology, for instance, the house is a symbol for the human body.

Takenouchi, Atsushi, born 1962 1
Prominent third-generation butoh performer in the lineage of Hijikata Tatsumi and Ohno Kazuo.

Takeuchi, Mika, born 1966 13
Third generation butoh dancer who started her own butoh institute in Sapporo in 2002, also a butoh dance therapist.

Tamano, Koichi and **Hiroko** 17
Anointed the "bow-legged Nijinsky" by his teacher Hijikata, Tamano Koichi and his wife Hiroko formed *Harupin-ha*, a dance company in Berkeley California that has performed internationally.

Theater of the Absurd 2
A form of theater representing the absurdity of human life through unconventional means; also a term used to identify a body of plays written primarily in France from the mid-1940s through the 1950s.

*Ukiyo-e** 14
Woodblock color prints, originating in Japan in the latter half of the seventeenth century and developing throughout the *Edo* period. These became fashionable in Europe and the United States by the late nineteenth century and in the early twentieth century. The French impressionists Edouard Manet, Edgar Degas, Henri de Toulouse-Lautrec, and Paul Gauguin, and American Mary Cassat shared an admiration of Ukiyo-e.

Waguri, Yukio 16
A disciple of Hijikata from 1972 until Hijikata's death in 1986. He currently tours in Japan and internationally presenting butoh work-shops, lectures and performances with his group *Butoh Kohzensha*. In 1992 he started the Hijikata Study Method Group, and in 1996 performed "*Butoh-Kaden*," a journey of seven *butoh-fu* worlds.

Waguri's exposition of Hijikata's *butoh-fu* is the first and, to date, only published source through which the public can access the process of Hijikata's *butoh-fu*.

Yang/Yin 20

1) Light and dark in the symbolism of China, originally the two sides of the mountain, sun and shadow, interpenetrating qualities at the foundation of perception and pervading all, male/female complements. 2) A Taoist conceptual scheme for explaining contrast and change.

Yoshioka, Yumiko, born 1953   17

Second generation butoh dancer and teacher, performing internationally, originally a member of the first female butoh dance company *Ariadone*. Now she pioneers butoh installations with visual art and teaches her dance methods internationally.

Zen* 13

A Buddhist religion originating in twelfth century China and developed later in Japan, teaching enlightenment through meditation, direct perception, and immediate insight. *Zen*, or in Chinese *Chan*, and Korean *Son*, designates a contemplative state of mind sometimes called "mindfulness." Disciples of Zen seek the Buddhist goal of "Suchness," or seeing the world just as it is with a mind that has no grasping thoughts or feelings. Zen exponents answer philosophic or spiritual questions through a method of non-symbolic direct pointing — the answer is the action and not what it represents.

Zen meditation 80

A Buddhist form of meditation practiced by students and adherents of Zen that uses sitting still, and sometimes counting techniques, *koans*, and postural protocols to still the mind. Forms vary slightly from one Zen practice to another, and sometimes include chanting as in Soto Zen. Dogen Zen advocates just sitting.

JAPANESE GLOSSARY
OF TERMS

Terms are spelled first using romanization followed by Japanese language writing systems. Ideograms, which are to some extent pictorial, originated in brush stroke calligraphy.

Ankoku Butoh（暗黒舞踏）
Aragoto（荒事）
Asubestoskan（アスベスト館）
Ashikawa Yoko（芦川羊子）
Butoh（舞踏）
Butoh-fu（舞踏譜）
Edo（江戸）
Eguchi Takaya（江口隆哉）
Heso to Genbaku（へそと原爆）
Harada Nobuo（原田伸雄）
Hijikata Tatsumi（土方巽）
Hijikata Tatsumi to nihonjin: Nikutai no hanran（土方巽と日本人：肉体の叛乱）
Hokohtai（歩行体）

Hosoe Eiko （細江英公）

Kamaitachi （鎌鼬）

Kamihitoe （紙一重）

Karada （体）

Kaze daruma （風だるま）

Koan （公安）

Konpaku （魂魄）

Ishii Baku （石井漠）

Jinen Butoh （じねん舞踏）

Kasai Akira （笠井叡）

Kinjiki （禁色）

La Argentina Sho （ラ・アルヘンチーナ頌）

Mishima Yukio （三島由紀夫）

Mu （無）

Nakajima Natsu （中嶋夏）

Niwa （庭）

Noguchi Taiso （野口体操）

Ohno Kazuo （大野一雄）

Ohno Yoshito （大野慶人）

Rose Colored Dance (Bara iro dansu) （バラ色ダンス）

Sankai Juku （山海塾）

Shiki no tame no nijuushichiban （四季のための二十七晩）

Shin （芯）

Suiren （睡蓮）

Takenouchi Atsushi （竹之内淳志）

Tohoku Kabuki （東北歌舞伎）

Ukiyo-e （浮世絵）

Waguri Yukio （和栗由紀夫）

Zen （禅）

BIBLIOGRAPHY

Arai, Masio (2003) *Hijikata Tatsumi Natsu-no arashi 2003, Hangi-daitoh-kan* (Hijikata Tatsumi, Summer Storm) Film and DVD, Tokyo: Daguerro Press.

Argentina Sho (Admiring La Argentina, 1977) choreographed and performed by Ohno Kazuo. Program notes translated by Barrett in 1988, Ohno Archives.

Baird, Bruce (2005) 'Buto and the Burden of History: Hijikata Tatsumi and *Nihonjin*' (Japan), unpublished doctoral dissertation, Philadelphia, PA: University of Pennsylvania.

Cahill, Thomas (2003) *Sailing the Wine-Dark Sea: Why the Greeks Matter*, New York: Anchor Books.

Esslin, Martin (1961) *The Theater of the Absurd*, Garden City, New York: Anchor Books, Double Day.

ETV Educational Television (2003) *96 Years Old: Lifelong Butohist, Dancing in My Hometown*, ETV Production, NHK, Tokyo.

Fisher, Elizabeth (1987) 'Butoh: The Secretly Perceived Made Visible,' unpublished masters thesis, New York: New York University.

Fraleigh, Sondra (1986) 'Interview with Ohno Kazuo', Yokohama, Japan, August 17, 1986.

—— (1987) *Dance and the Lived Body*, Pittsburgh, PA: University of Pittsburgh Press.

—— (1999) *Dancing into Darkness: Butoh, Zen, and Japan*, Pittsburgh, PA: University of Pittsburgh Press.

—— (2003) Interview with Takenouchi Atsushi, Broellin Castle, Broellin, Germany, *EXIT Butoh Festival*, August 15, 2003.

—— (2004) *Dancing Identity: Metaphysics in Motion*, Pittsburgh, PA: University of Pittsburgh Press.

—— (2005) 'Spacetime and Mud in Butoh', in *Performing Nature: Explorations in Ecology and the Arts*, edited by Gabriella Giannachi and Nigel Stewart, Oxford: Peter Lang, 327–44.

Genet, Jean (1969) *The Thief's Journal*, translated by Bernard Frechtman, New York: Grove Press.

Goda, Nario (1983) '*Ankoku Buto ni Tsuite*' (on Ankoku Buto), in Hanaga Mitsutoshi (ed.), *Butoh*, Tokyo: Gendaishokan, unpaginated.

—— (1987) '*Hijikata butoh sakuhin noto 2*' (Hijikata Butoh Work Notes 2), *Asubesutokan tsushin* 5, October: 41–2.

Goodman, David (1971) 'New Japanese Theatre', *The Drama Review* 15: 154–68.

Guth, Christine (1996) *Japanese Art of the Edo Period*, London: Weidenfeld and Nicolson.

Hijikata, Tatsumi (1959) Program Notes for *Kinjiki*, 1959 *Zen'nihon buyo kyokai shinjin koen* (All Japan Dance Association New Face Performance).

—— (1984) Letter to Natsu Nakajima, "To My Comrade," Fraleigh's private collection.

—— (2000a) 'Inner Material/Material' (*Naka no sozai/sozai*, 1960), in Kurihara Nanako (ed.), 'Hijikata Tatsumi: The Words of Butoh', translated by Jacqueline S. Ruyak and Kurihara Nanako, *The Drama Review* (Spring) 44, 1: 36–42. Article originally published in July of 1960 as '*Naka no sozai/sozai*', a pamphlet for Hijikata DANCE EXPERIENCE *no kai* (recital).

—— (2000b) 'To Prison' (*Keimusho e*, 1961), in Kurihara Nanako (ed.), 'Hijikata Tatsumi: The Words of Butoh', translated by Jacqueline S. Ruyak and Kurihara Nanako, *The Drama Review* (Spring) 44, 1: 43–8. Article originally published in January of 1961 as '*Keimusho e*' in *Mita Bungaku* (The Mita Literature): 45–9.

—— (2000c) 'From Being Jealous of a Dog's Vein' (*Inu*, 1969), in Kurihara Nanako (ed.), 'Hijikata Tatsumi: The Words of Butoh', translated by Jacqueline S. Ruyak and Kurihara Nanako, *The Drama Review* (Spring) 44, 1: 56–9. Article originally published in May of 1969 as '*Inu no jomyakuni shitto suru koto kara*' in *Bijutsu Techo*.

—— (2000d) 'Wind Daruma' (*Kaze daruma*, 1985), in Kurihara Nanako (ed.), 'Hijikata Tatsumi: The Words of Butoh', translated by Jacqueline S. Ruyak and Kurihara Nanako, *The Drama Review* (Spring) 44, 1: 71–9. Originally published as '*Kaze daruma*', in *Gendaishi techo* in May of 1985. Hijikata's *Kaze daruma* is a speech originally titled '*Suijakutai no saishu*' (Collection of Emaciated Body), given the night before the Butoh Festival in February of 1985.

—— (2000e) 'Fragments of Glass: A Conversation between Hijikata, Tatsumi and Suzuki Tadashi', in Kurihara Nanako (ed.), 'Hijikata Tatsumi: The words of Butoh', translated by Jacqueline S. Ruyak and Kurihara Nanako, *The Drama Review*, (Spring) 44, 1: 62–70. Article originally published in April 1977 as '*Ketsujo to shite no gengo-Shintai no kasetsu*' (Language as Lack and Temporary construction of the Body) in Gendaishi Techo.

Hijikata, Tatsumi Archives (2000) *Hijikata Tatsumi butoh shiryōshū dai ippo* (Hijikata Tatsumi Butoh Materials), Tokyo: Research Center for Arts & Arts Administration, Keio University.

Holborn, Mark and Ethan Hoffman (eds) (1987) *Butoh: Dance of the Dark Soul*, New York: Aperture.

Hosoe, Eikoh (1969) *Kamaitachi* (Sickle-Weasel), Tokyo: Gendaishichosha.

Igarashi, Yoshikuni (2000) *Bodies of Memory: Narratives of War in Postwar Japanese Culture, 1945–1970*, Princeton, NJ: Princeton University Press.

Ives, Colta (1974) *The Great Wave: The Influence of Japanese Woodcuts on French Prints*, New York: Metropolitan Museum of Art.

Kasai, T. (1999) 'A Butoh Dance Method for psychosomatic exploration', *Memoirs of the Hokkaido Institute of Technology* 27: 309–16.

Kasai, Toshiharu and Takeuchi, Mika (2001) 'Mind–Body Learning by the Butoh Dance Method', *Proceedings from the 36th Annual Conference of American Dance Therapy Association*, Raleigh, NC, October 11–14, 2001.

Klein, Susan (1988) *Ankoku Butoh: The Premodern and Postmodern Influences on the Dance of Utter Darkness*, Ithaca, NY: Cornell University Press.

Kuniyoshi, Kazuko (1990) *Performing Arts in Japan Now: Butoh in the Late 1980s*, Tokyo: The Japan Foundation.

—— (2000) *Ichikawa Miyabi: Mirukoto no kyori, dansu no kiseki* (Ichikawa Miyabi: The Perception of Distance in Dance), Tokyo: Shinshokan.

—— (2002) *Yume no ishō: Kioku no tsubo* (Dance and Modernism), Tokyo: Shinshokan.

—— (2004a) *Contemporary Dance in Japan: New Wave in Dance and Butoh After the 1990s*, Tokyo: Arts Midwest.

—— (2004b) '*Hijikata Tatsumi to ankoku butoh: Miidasareta nikutai*' (Hijikata Tatsumi and his Ankoku Butoh: Dance of Darkness – The Retrieved Bodies), in Taro *Okamoto Musuem of Arts* and Keio University Research Center for the Arts and Arts Administration (eds), Tokyo: Keiogiju-kudaigakushuppankai.

Kurihara, Nanako (1996) 'The Most Remote Thing in the Universe: Critical Analysis of Hijikata Tatsumi's Butoh Dance,' unpublished doctoral dissertation, New York: New York University.

—— (2000) 'Hijikata Tatsumi: The Words of Butoh', *The Drama Review* (Spring) 44, 1: 12–33.

Laage, Joan (1993) 'Embodying the Spirit: The Significance of the Body in the Contemporary Japanese Dance Movement of Butoh', unpublished doctoral dissertation, Denton, TX: Texas Woman's University.

Lee, William (2002) 'Kabuki as National Culture: A Critical Survey of Japanese Kabuki Scholarship', in Samuel Leiter (ed.) *A Kabuki Reader: History and Performance*, London: M.E. Sharpe.

Matsubara, Saika and other commentators (1998) '*Hijikata Tatsumi: the CoMPaSSioNaTe SouL BiRD comes to unfurl its rustling SKeLeTaL WiNGS*'.

Tape and booklet, ARIA Disques in Japan. Tape and booklet based on Hijikata's original spoken monologue in 1976.

McGee, Micki (1986) 'An Avant-garde Becomes an Institution', *High Performance* 33: 49.

Mikami, Kayo (1993) *Utsuwa to shite no shintai* (Body as Vessel), Tokyo: Namishobō.

Motofuji, Akiko (1990) *Hijikata Tatsumi to tomo ni* (With Hijikata Tatsumi), Tokyo: Chikumashobō.

Munroe, Alexandra (1994) *Scream Against the Sky: Japanese Art After 1945*, New York: Harry N. Abrams.

Nakajima, Natsu (1997) '*Ankoku Butoh*', Speech at Fu Jen University Decade Conference, *Feminine Spirituality in Theatre, Opera, and Dance,* Taipei (October 1997), translated by Lee Chee-Keng in 1997, revised by Elizabeth Langley in 2002.

Nakamura, Fumiaki (1993) *Butoh no oshie* (Teachings of butoh), in Takashi Tachiki (ed.), *Ten-nin keraku: Ohno Kazuo no sekai (Ten-nin keraku: The World of Ohno Kazuo)*, Tokyo: Seikyusha: 11–41.

Nakamura, Tamah (2001) 'Interview with Harada Nobuo', Fukuoka, Japan, July 6, 2001.

—— (2005) 'Interview with Ohno Yoshito', Yokohama, Japan, March 19, 2005.

—— (2006) 'Beyond Performance in Japanese Butoh Dance: Embodying Re-Creation of Self and Social Identities', unpublished doctoral dissertation, Santa Barbara, CA: Fielding Graduate University.

Noguchi, Hiroyuki (2004) 'The Idea of the Body in Japanese Culture and its Dismantlement', *International Journal of Sport and Health Science* 2: 8–24.

Noguchi, Michizo (1996) *Genshoseimeitai to shiteno ningen: Noguchitaiso no riron* (The Theory of Noguchi Exercises: Humans as the Agent of Life), Tokyo: Iwanamishoten.

Ohno, Kazuo (1986) 'Selections from the Prose of Ohno Kazuo', *The Drama Review* 30, 2: 156–62.

—— (1992a) *Dessin*, Kushiro, Hokkaido: Ryokugeisha.

—— (1992b) *Ohno Kazuo butoh fu: Goten sora o tobu* (Ohno Kazuo on Butoh: The Palace Soars Through the Sky), Tokyo: Shichōsha.

—— (1997) *Keiko no kotoba* (Words of Workshop), Tokyo: Firumuātosha.

—— (2001) *Beauty and Strength*. NHK Video Software.

—— (2002) *Ishikari no hanamagari* (The Ishikari River's Hooked-nose Salmon). Karinsha.

Ohno, Kazuo and Ohno, Yoshito (2004) *Kazuo Ohno's World from Within and Without*, translated by John Barrett, Wesleyan, CT: Wesleyan University Press.

Ohno, Kazuo with Ulrike Dopfer and Axel Tangerding (1994) 'The Body is Already the Universe: Dance on the Borderlines of Death – a Conversation with Kazuo Ohno in Yokohama in March 1994', *Ballet International* 8, 9: 52–5.

Ohno, Yoshito (1999) *Ohno Kazuo: Tamashii no kate* (Ohno Kazuo: Bread/Food for the Soul), Tokyo: Firumuātosha.

Osaki, Shinichiro (1998) 'Body and Place: Action in Postwar Art in Japan' in Paul Schimmel (ed.) *Out of Actions: Between Performance and the Object 1949–1979*, New York: Thames and Hudson.

Ozawa-De Silva, C. (2002) 'Beyond the body/mind? Japanese contemporary thinkers on alternative sociologies of the body', *Body and Society* 8, 2: 21–38.

Sagner-Duchting, Karin (1999) *Monet at Giverny*, Munich: Prestel Verlag.

Sakurai, Keisuke, Itoh, Seiko, and Oshikiri, Shin-ichi (1998) *Nishiazabu dansu kyōshitsu* (Seminar of Dance at Nishiazabu), Tokyo: Hakusuisha.

Sas, Miryam (1999) *Fault Lines, Cultural Memory and Japanese Surrealism*, Stanford, CA: Stanford University Press.

Schechner, Richard (1986) 'Interview with Kazuo Ohno', *The Drama Review* 30, 2: 163–9.

Scheyer, Ernst (1970) 'The Shapes of Space: The Art of Mary Wigman and Oskar Schlemmer', *Dance Perspectives* 41, New York: Dance Perspectives Foundation.

Senda, Akihiko (1977) 'Fragments of Glass: A Conversation Between Hijikata Tatsumi and Suzuki Tadashi', *The Drama Review*: 62–70.

Slater, Lizzie (1986) 'The Dead Begin to Run: Kazuo Ohno and Butoh Dance', *Dance Theatre Journal* (Winter): 6–10.

Stewart, Nigel (1998) 'Re-Languaging the Body: Phenomeno-logical Description and the Dance Image', in *Performance Research,* 'On Place' (Summer) 3, 2: 42–53.

Strom, Kirsten (2004) '"Avant-Garde of What?": Surrealism Reconceived as Political Culture', *The Journal of Aesthetics and Art Criticism* (Winter) 62, 1: 37–49.

Tachiki, Takashi (1993) *Ten-nin keraku: Ohno Kazuo no sekai* (*Ten-nin keraku:* The World of Ohno Kazuo), Tokyo: Seikyusha.

Tanizaki, Junichiro (1977) *In Praise of Shadows*, translated by Thomas J. Harper and Edward G. Seidensticker, Foreword by Charles Moore, Stony Creek, CT: Leete's Island Books.

Taro Okamoto Museum of Art, Kawasaki City and Keio University Research Center for the Arts and Arts Administration, Tokyo (eds) (2004) *Hijikata Tatsumi no butoh: Nikutai no shururearizumu shintai no ontoroji* (Tatsumi Hijikata's Butoh: Surrealism of the Flesh, Ontology of the Body), Tokyo: Keio Gijukudaigakushuppankai.

Toland, John (1970) *The Rising Sun: The Decline and Fall of the Japanese Empire 1936–1945*, New York: Penguin.

Tschudin, Jean-Jacques (1999) '*Danjuro's Katsureki-geki* "Realistic Theatre" and the Meiji Theatre Reform Movement', *Japan Forum* 11, 1: 83–94.

Viala, Jean and Sekine, Nourit Masson (1988) *Butoh: Shades of Darkness*, Tokyo: Shufunotomo.

Waguri, Yukio (1998) *Butoh-Kaden*, CD-Rom and booklet, Tokushima: Justsystem.

Wurmli, Kurt (2004) 'Images of Dance and the Dance of Images: A Research Report on Hijikata Tatsumi's Butoh', commissioned by Keio University, Tokyo, unpublished manuscript.

Yoshioka, Minoru (1987) *Hijikata Tatsumi ko* (On Hijikata Tatsumi), Tokyo: Chikumashobo.

Yuasa, Y. (1987) *The Body: Toward an Eastern Mind–Body Theory*, New York: State University of New York Press.

INDEX

Page numbers in **bold** refer to illustrations.

democracy, Hijikata on 29, 44
Denishawn 16, 149
desire 74
Dessin 63, 64
Dionysus 86–7
disappearance 52, 106–7
Divine 23, 32, 90
Duncan, Isadora 17, 30, 155

eclecticism 16, 149
Edo period 11, 15, 149
Eguchi Takaya 9, 14, 20, 21, 25, 33,
    149, 150
Eiko 29
emergence 104
emotion 15–16, 30
empathy 3, 149
emptiness 16, 63, 72, 104
Endo Tadashi 17, 40, 102, 104, 133
erotic dance 8, 20, 34, 40, 80, 81
Esslin, Martin 48, 49
ethnography 16, 37, 149
ethnology 46
ethos 72, 149
eurythmy 17, 152
Europe: influence of butoh in 2, 40; Ohno
    Kazuo tours 34, 35; Takenouchi in 39;
    Ukiyo-e woodcuts fashionable in 15
evil 87
Excerpts from Genet 84
existentialism 74, 149, 155
EXIT Dance Research and Exchange
    Project 118
experience: art as 45; dance as 72, 73–5,
    78
expressionism 2, 3, 74, 150; German
    14, 15–16, 36, 48, 150; *see also Neue
    Tanz*
expressiveness 2, 29, 30, 62

facial expressions 2, 29, 30, 62
floating 16

flowers 67, 97–8, 114–15
*Flowers and Birds, Wind and Moon (Ka Cho
    Fu Getsu)* 35
forms 16, 31, 56
'Fragments of Glass' 52
Fraleigh, Sondra 16, 37, 43, 55, 68–9,
    102, 105
France: *Admiring La Argentina* in 34, 93,
    94; butoh procession in Avignon 129
Fuerio, Antonio 93–4

Genet, Jean 45, 90; influence of 8, 84,
    150
Germany 20, 40; *see also* expressionism,
    German
Goda Nario 8, 46, 78, 79
GooSayTen 124, 154
Graham, Martha 72, 155, 157
grotesque gestures 21, 76
grounded walking 16
Grupo de Teatro Macunaima 93
gyrations 16

haiku 40, 62, 65, 118, 150
hair-splitting 13, 128–9
hair-splitting difference 115–16, 128
Hakodate City 25, 36
Hanagami Naoto 89
'Hanging Body' 16, 120–3
Harada Nobuo 138, **139**, 140, 150–1;
    DANCE EXPERIENCES 141–2
Harupin-ha dance company 17
healing 39
Hearn, Lafcadio 36
Heaven: We walk on Eternity 24
Heraclitus 31
Heso to Genbaku (Navel and Atomic Bomb)
    13
Hicks, Greg 111–12
Hijikata Study Method Group 143
Hijikata Tatsumi 1–2, 3, 18; death of 47,
    48; influence of childhood 19;

Related titles from Routledge

Theatre Histories:
An Introduction

Edited by Philip B. Zarrilli, Bruce McConachie, Gary Jay Williams and Carol Fisher Sorgenfrei

'This book will significantly change theatre education.'
Janelle Reinelt, *University of California, Irvine*

Theatre Histories: An Introduction is a radically new way of looking at both the way history is written and the way we understand performance.

The authors provide beginning students and teachers with a clear, exciting journey through centuries of European, North and South American, African and Asian forms of theatre and performance.

Challenging the standard format of one-volume theatre history texts, they help the reader think critically about this vibrant field through fascinating yet plain-speaking essays and case studies.

Among the topics covered are:

- representation and human expression
- interpretation and critical approaches
- historical method and sources
- communication technologies
- colonization
- oral and literate cultures
- popular, sacred and elite forms of performance.

Keeping performance and culture very much centre stage, *Theatre Histories: An Introduction* is compatible with standard play anthologies, full of insightful pedagogical apparatus, and comes accompanied by web site resources.

ISBN10: 0–415–22727–5 (hbk)
ISBN10: 0–415–22728–3 (pbk)

ISBN13: 978–0–415–22727–8 (hbk)
ISBN13: 978–0–415–22728–5 (pbk)

Available at all good bookshops
For ordering and further information please visit:
www.routledge.com

eBooks – at www.eBookstore.tandf.co.uk

A library at your fingertips!

eBooks are electronic versions of printed books. You can store them on your PC/laptop or browse them online.

They have advantages for anyone needing rapid access to a wide variety of published, copyright information.

eBooks can help your research by enabling you to bookmark chapters, annotate text and use instant searches to find specific words or phrases. Several eBook files would fit on even a small laptop or PDA.

NEW: Save money by eSubscribing: cheap, online access to any eBook for as long as you need it.

Annual subscription packages

We now offer special low-cost bulk subscriptions to packages of eBooks in certain subject areas. These are available to libraries or to individuals.

For more information please contact webmaster.ebooks@tandf.co.uk

We're continually developing the eBook concept, so keep up to date by visiting the website.

www.eBookstore.tandf.co.uk

Lightning Source UK Ltd.
Milton Keynes UK
UKOW06f0338120316

270070UK00013B/226/P

9 780415 354394